Mental Me

Fears, Flashbacks and Fixations

Justin Rollins

≋ WATERSIDE PRESS

'Justin Rollins is a young writer of raw, authentic and exciting talent.

He has used it in *Mental Me* to take his readers on a searing, page-turning, roller coaster ride through one of the darkest jungles in the Criminal Justice System — the incarceration of mentally ill young offenders.

Paranoic violence, brutal beatings, PTSD nightmares and OCD obsessions, leading to attempts at arson or suicide erupt across the landscape of this story like flame-throwing volcanoes.

Yet, Justin Rollins, who as a teenage prisoner wrote 600 poems between nervous breakdowns, clings to his unlikely dream of becoming a successful author. How he made this dream come true is an epic saga of horror and hope. It deserves to be a best seller.'

Jonathan Aitken

Mental Me: Fears, Flashbacks and Fixations
Justin Rollins

ISBN 978-1-914603-11-2 (Paperback)
ISBN 978-1-914603-12-9 (EPUB ebook)
ISBN 978-1-914603-13-6 (PDF ebook)

Cover design © 2022 Waterside Press. Photo of the author Nick Cornwall.

Main UK distributor Gardners Books, 1 Whittle Drive, Eastbourne, BN23 6QH. Tel: (+44) 01323 521777; sales@gardners.com; www.gardners.com

North American distribution Ingram Book Company, One Ingram Blvd, La Vergne, TN 37086, USA. Tel: (+1) 615 793 5000; inquiry@ingramcontent.com

Cataloguing In-Publication Data A catalogue record for this book can be obtained from the British Library.

Printed by Severn, Gloucester, UK.

Published 2022 by
Waterside Press Ltd
Sherfield Gables
Sherfield on Loddon, Hook
Hampshire RG27 0JG.

Telephone +44(0)1256 882250
Online catalogue WatersidePress.co.uk
Email enquiries@watersidepress.co.uk

Table of Contents

Foreword by Noel 'Razor' Smith

The writing of Justin Rollins is visceral, it hits you right in the gut with the power of a knock-out punch from a heavyweight boxer. No prisoners are taken in this testament to mental health and the adverse effects of imprisonment from a young age. Anyone who has been unlucky enough to spend any time in a UK prison will know the toll it takes on their mental health. Many prisoners are 'sectioned' (under the Mental Health Act) every year and our prisons are hotbeds of paranoia, psychotic episodes, and serious violence. Treatment and help for those with mental health problems in our prison system is almost non-existent, until the prisoner takes action and causes problems for the system, then they will be 'dealt with'. Either they get dosed-up on medication (known as the 'liquid cosh') and isolated in punishment blocks, or they are sectioned and sent to secure hospitals. The poor treatment of mentally-ill people by the justice system in general and the prison system in particular, is shameful.

Justin Rollins' book is long overdue and should be required reading for those who run our criminal justice system and who fail to help the disturbed young people in their charge. Justin has lived through it all and survived, but still carries the mental and physical scars to this day. He takes us through those hopeless and desperate years when thoughts of suicide and self-harm were a daily mantra in his head. The effect of imprisonment on this already mentally fragile youth are there to be witnessed by the reader.

All of this makes for a very revealing if disturbing book, and harrowing read. But it is a great story and not to be missed though please prepare yourself for the author's 'knock-out' punches!

The author
Photograph by Nick Cornwall © 2022.

About the author

Justin Rollins grew-up on the streets of South London and was at one-time a leader of a graffiti gang. Ten years ago following publication of his acclaimed *The Lost Boyz: The Dark Side of Graffiti* (Waterside Press, 2011) he found himself a 'go to' expert and speaker on gang and knife crime, including at colleges and universities where that book became a key text for criminology students and others. Having served time for violence in his youth, he now works to encourage young people stay away from street crime, gangs, drugs and criminal activity. His struggle to overcome long-standing mental health issues (that affected his offending especially) is the subject of this new book.

The author of the Foreword

Noel 'Razor' Smith is the best-selling author of *A Few Kind Words and a Loaded Gun: The Autobiography of a Career Criminal* (Penguin, 2005) and *The Dirty Dozen: The Real Story of the Rise and Fall of London's Most Feared Armed Robbery Gang* (John Blake, 2020). As a journalist he has written for the national press and works for the prison newspaper *Inside Time*.

Acknowledgements

First and foremost, my beautiful Dukes.

Secondly, the whole of team No Dog: Darius Norowzian, Todd Von Joel, James Byrne, Jaime Winstone, Tyler Brindle, Daniel Phelan, Kaliffe Kelly, Richard Amado, Ollie Nice, Richard McDonald and all of the others involved in the project.

My special thanks are also due to Tony Wood, Big Hyper, Dean Smith, Sean McGirr, Luke Mcilroy, Sean London, Sterling, David Williams, Pey Moghaddam, Billy VIP Graffiti, Killa Kela, Mental Met, Dems, Wavey Garms, Professor David Wilson, The Reverend Jonathan Aitken, Dr Tim Turner, S J McClelland, Karen Mason, Simon Scott and Nick Cornwall.

And finally, to Bryan Gibson and Noel 'Razor' Smith for believing in my writing.

Justin Rollins
March 2022

For Gabriella, Skyla and Lorenzo

Publisher's note

The views and opinions in this book are those of the author and not necessarily shared by the publisher. Readers should draw their own conclusions concerning the possibility of alternative views or accounts.

The author wishes to emphasise that although based on real events details may have been changed or adapted, especially where these relate to names, places or descriptions of criminal activity.

CHAPTER 1

My First Taste of a Real Prison

From age eleven I spent most of my time as a runaway. By age 14 I found myself leader of a South London street gang, The Warriorz. Trapped in a chaotic lifestyle and too young to comprehend the trauma involved, my mental health fell into decline. The violence took its toll and sadly by age 18 I'd lost my best friend Joe Smith to those streets. With nowhere to turn after years of alienating myself from normal society I decided to 'check out.' Armed with a meat cleaver for protection from rival gangs I made my way onto a tube train. I planned to commit a robbery and hoped I'd get arrested ... or die in the process.

One of my intended victims overpowered me and chopped me with the meat cleaver cutting my jaw and hand. I survived my act of madness and got my wish of leaving the chaos I knew so well. But if I thought it would bring any kind of peace I was deluded. What happened next is that I entered a whole new world of mental challenges and desperation after being sentenced to four-and-a-half years in prison.

I was taken to Her Majesty's Prison High Down not far from my home in Carshalton in Surrey. There with only my mind and four walls for company I lay on my bed worried about what the future had in store for me. With at least three years to serve it felt like a lifetime to a young man. 'I won't cope,' I thought anxiously, but I also considered myself lucky that I was just up the road from my family and friends. One week later all this changed when my cell door opened and I heard a voice shout, 'Pack your bags.'

As the prison van left High Down and made its way through the area I knew so well it dawned on me this was it. I was locked-up in this tiny moving cell watching my manor and life fade away, and fast, through a tiny, scratched window. The ride in the sweat box was uncomfortable and seemed to take forever as we headed up an endless motorway and my days as a gang leader seemed a distant memory as we travelled far away from home. 'I won't ever set eyes on my old stomping ground again,' I thought as Woodhill came into view.

Woodhill Prison near Milton Keynes in Buckinghamshire was where some of the most dangerous offenders in the entire country were held. Until then I never even knew Milton Keynes existed and to a South Londoner it seemed as if it was in the far North. Part of the prison had been turned into a maximum-security facility and I'd heard it housed prisoners such as Robert Stewart who murdered another prisoner, Zahid Mubarek, in Zahid's cell at Feltham Young Offender Institution (YOI); and the notorious Charles Bronson dubbed by the media 'the most violent prisoner in Britain.' The maximum-security wing was 'a prison within a prison' and a damning report by HM Chief Inspector of Prisons had criticised the conditions in its close supervision unit, saying its inmates were deprived of mental stimulation and human contact.

Woodhill also catered for other types of prisoners: adults, young offenders, category A inmates and 'supergrasses.' A special unit held some of the most high-profile informers in the criminal underworld. Nine out of ten of these had a large bounty on their heads. They were 'dead men walking'; and it was far too risky to allow them on normal prison locations, not even with an alias. Even prison officers working on that unit never knew their names, they were just called Bloggs 1, Bloggs 2 and so on. They had special meals for fear they'd be poisoned. These men had been responsible for destroying major criminal networks and sending gangsters and others involved in organized crime to prison to serve long sentences. Those out to get them may have been 'top dogs' but we can't really call them organized when one of their own had turned informer just to receive a lighter sentence. On their release supergrasses would disappear into witness protection programmes with new identities and 'safe' accommodation well away from their old patches.

So, as you can see this was a weird and wonderful place. I was allocated a double cell on the wing for young offenders. To be honest I hated sharing a cell, it was a nightmare, two inmates locked-up in a what was originally a single for one, with a bunk bed, twenty-three hours a day. Within a day you'd have worked out your cellmate's bad points. For example, his feet might smell, he might snore, and he might have hygiene problems. Now if I was to tell you that you stank and needed a wash you'd not be happy. So, you had to play the game carefully. Insulting a guy who I knew absolutely nothing about could easily lead him to attack me whilst I was sleeping. I've always liked my own company and could become a bit of a loner at times so sharing was not for me. I did have a few decent cellmates at times though, but when you become a bit too friendly, or the jokes get out of hand, it can end in blows.

Woodhill was different to London jails in terms of its prisoner population, most of the inmates seemed to be Northerners or came from the Midlands. There were a lot of Birmingham and Liverpool men and they in turn saw the jail as a 'Southern' prison. I'm sure they had a bigger drug problem at Woodhill than in London. Everybody seemed to be on heroin, something I hadn't noticed while spending time in custody in the capital. Inmates were going cold turkey and would exchange prescribed medication, such as anti-depressants and sleeping tablets, for tobacco.

Whilst in prison I smoked a lot, and when you are out of tobacco inside and desperate for a smoke you can turn crazy. If someone was supposed to save you a bit of their roll-up and they or somebody else smoked it, you could easily find yourself fighting over that. The roll-up might be just a butt like you'd see on the floor walking down the street that you wouldn't give a second thought to, but in prison two inmates could be slugging it out in the showers over that dog end.

I used to take medication to protect my stomach lining due to an ulcer. I'd take one capsule of a prescription drug called Losec, or Lansoprazole, when my tobacco ran out, and I was clucking like a heroin addict for a smoke. I'd pretend to somebody that my pills were anti-depressants then exchange them for tobacco, promising the addict that the tablets I was giving them would give them an almighty buzz, which would take them away from the reality of prison life. Later, smoking a roll-up, I'd shout out of my cell window, 'Bruv, how's the tablet? On one occasion a Northern voice replied, 'Fucking great, mate, I'm off my nut' when in reality his stomach was just getting a bit of protection. Now that's a mild story linked to the drug problem in prison. I'm about to tell you one that's stomach churning, so you might need to pop a pill or two yourself before you read on.

A fragile heroin addict four doors down from my cell had recently had a visit from some fellow heroin addict friends. They'd smuggled him in a small bag passing it to him during a visit. He got back to his cell and was in 'skag-head heaven.' At first, he kept it secret from his cellmate who also had a raging habit, but once the fragile addict's clucking got out of control he pulled out the gear and shared a bit with his cellmate. He then placed the remaining heroin up his anus to hide it from the prison officers and safe keeping, so he thought.

Next day his cellmate was raging for another hit, but when the fragile addict refused to share more an argument broke out. The raging addict finally lost it. He told two of his mates and they decided to rob the fragile addict. As the fragile one sat in his cell alone the door burst open. His cellmate and two of skaghead friends were standing there and he quickly realised this wasn't going to be a friendly call. They ordered him to hand over the bag of heroin as they set about him. He swore he'd used it all, but the cellmate knew he was lying, then realised it was up the fragile addict's backside. So by now you're getting where this story is going, I'm tensing just thinking about it. Two of them held the fragile addict on the floor whilst the raging addict pulled down the fragile lad's trousers and armed with a plastic spoon began to dig for treasure. If you don't know, heroin is brown in colour. To be honest, I don't know how they worked out what was what, but they got their prize and scarpered.

Heroin is a vile drug, for somebody to rather go through that than hand over their stash and for any man to do that to another just to get a buzz, well I'll leave you to work it out. The raging addict wanted that buzz so much he never even considered that he still had to share the cell with his victim. So, to all of you who have the image of a prison as a hotel you are very wrong, that is just one story we all now know about. I dread to think about the ones that remain untold.

The High Down Healthcare Unit where I spent a few months was chaotic to say the least. But I handled my new environment pretty well and there weren't too many cutthroats like in a London jail, to be honest I saw my new fellow inmates as country bumpkins and really needed to be around my own crowd. I got talking to a guy from Walthamstow in East London called Roger. Apart from Roger and me there were only a couple of other London boys, so we stuck together. I persuaded a prison officer to put us together in a new double cell. He was probably my best cellmate. He didn't irritate me and we always had a laugh.

After the association period we'd be locked in our cells for the evening. That's when the inmates turned into wild animals in their cages. Stereos would be on fall blast, people screaming out of the windows, doors being kicked and all out of boredom. We young offenders enjoyed the odd spot of fly-tipping; any rubbish would get thrown out of our cell windows. If you were to walk below outside it would literally be knee deep in stuff. So come night-time we'd light a bit of newspaper and drop it down onto the waste, and as evening went on there would be fires going on everywhere. Looking through those bars seeing the prison grounds lit up from the fires gave me a strange feeling. I'd howl out of the window like a wolf and before you knew it you had maybe 50 young prisoners at their windows doing the same, screaming out animal sounds. You had little dogs barking, big dogs growling, cats meowing, sheep, cows, monkeys, birds squawking and the sound of every other creature you can imagine. Hearing those crazy sounds whilst watching the screws trying to extinguish the fires would give me an overwhelming feeling of madness. My environment was mad and even though Roger and me had a good time as cellmates, like the rest of my friendships and life it always ended badly ... or extremely badly!

I'd always let Roger know that I was a bit crazy, by telling him stories of my messed-up life with my teenage gang back on the South London streets. Now he was about to see for himself. One ritual on the young offender unit was to kick the hell out of your cell door once 'Eastenders' finished. So, like any other night we started to kick our doors. But as me and Roger kicked harder and harder to impress each other, I decided to pick up a chair and start smashing it against the door. The sound became deafening as the whole unit smashed with their chairs too. By accident I shattered the glass in the door. High on adrenalin, Roger grabbed the chair and started to smash the window all the way through. Once we'd calmed down we realised we were going to get nicked and end up in the punishment block.

Then I came up with an idea of pure genius. I was a self-harmer and I'd been cutting and scratching wounds into my arms since I was a teenager. My plan was this. I'd slice my arm a little, Roger would ring the buzzer and inform the screws he was so scared of what I was doing he'd hit the chair against the door to alert them, accidently breaking the glass. Well, come on then smart arse, what would your plan have been?

I pulled out my razor and started to cut my arm, but sometimes you could say that I go over the top. As Roger saw the blood pouring-out he got scared. But my psychotic mode was kicking-off and I couldn't stop now. I'd crossed the line. Roger alerted the screws and they ordered us out of the cell; he left, and I screamed to the screws to fuck off. A nurse tried to enter the cell to calm me down, so I picked up the chair and threw it at him, he quickly ducked and slammed the door firmly shut. I was running this show now, or so I thought in my state of mind.

I turned-up my music and tied a noose around my neck. Then I proceeded to slice deep wounds in my wrists, and I covered my face with blood. I was insane at that stage and very unstable and dangerous, the years of trauma I'd witnessed as a child were coming out. With no understanding of my thoughts, feelings or flashbacks I'd completely lost control. To the screws looking through the smashed glass it must have seemed like an image from a horror movie.

As I sat at the back of my cell screaming abuse at the officers, the door suddenly opened. My mind was already in a daze, and for a split second I didn't realise who or what was standing there. Then I realised it was a 15-stone female officer with a riot shield. 'Fuck me,' I thought, 'I'm hallucinating.' She ran at me like a raging bull, smashing me to the floor. Then she hit me with the shield several times, rested it on me and sat on top of it. I grabbed hold of a bed leg and pulled myself under the bunk.

As the cell filled with screws I felt an almighty pain in my ribs and one of them continued to kick me as they dragged me out. I was held on the floor on the landing with my arms behind my back, in prisoner slang 'bent up.' The screws use this tactic which is very effective and extremely painful but as I was in full mental mode I told them I enjoyed that experience, until one of them pulled my arms so far up my back I cried in agony.

They dragged me through the unit and as thy did so half of the inmates started smashing in their doors and screaming abuse: 'Let him go you bastards ... dirty bullies.' I then noticed the female screw who'd done me with the riot shield, she was so big and ugly, if I'd asked her to fight me one-to-one then I'm sure she'd still have knocked me clean out. I was dragged through the prison grounds without a clue where I was heading. Suddenly we came to a halt; I was then dragged into this strange looking building and taken into a separate part of it that had been boarded-up for some reason.

'I'm home,' I thought. I was back on another healthcare unit, this time in the cages, and there were three altogether. A cage is a twenty-four-seven observation cell designed to prevent suicides or for other problem prisoners. Cages have a barred area beyond and outside the usual steel door. I was slung into the middle one. By the cages there was a table full of paperwork, a television screen, and a female officer. The cell itself was almost empty, an eerie, dark and grimy environment. Someone was observing from outside and my only way to regain some control was to try to make his evening as miserable as possible. I wanted to seek revenge for them hurting my arms so I covered myself in a smelly white blanket smeared with my own blood so you could only see my face. For an hour or two I walked around in a circle mumbling strange things and I could see the fear in the screw's eyes as he looked on. In reality and apart from the kicks and force used those officers' actions were right. I'd been pointing a blade and throwing chairs around. I was dangerous and they had no option but to bring in their female version of Arnold Schwarzenegger to sort me out.

I eventually got my head down and fell asleep. I woke next morning, my body battered and bruised, miles from home. There were a couple of feet between the bars and the cell door behind it which was kept permanently open, so I could walk out to the bars and have a nose around. To my left I saw part of the unit was hidden from the rest of it, but I thought nothing of it. To my right I noticed the television again and wondered why I never had one. I then went back to bed and thought of my new situation, when I suddenly had a strange feeling of madness in my soul again, and for some strange reason I was drawn back to the bars. I began to scan for my neighbour's cell card to read his name. That feeling of madness was once again correct; my eyes stared at the card in disbelief. It read 'HUNTLEY CAT A.' This was not like the killers I'd met on the wing. I was now locked-up next to one of the most hated men in the country who'd killed two young girls. 'If this man had been placed on a normal prison location he'd surely not have lasted the day,' I told myself.

I sat there and questioned my crazy life telling myself this could only happen to me. I wanted to be mad and bad so much throughout my childhood, it was my shield, my armour. I wanted it so much more then my friends that I became the leader of our gang. But now I was alone, my gang were miles away and I hadn't heard from them for months. It was like someone was saying to me, 'Listen mate, you wanted craziness in your life, now deal with it.'

A wise man once told me, 'Don't be the mad one in your gang you'll end up very lonely.' I sat there lonely, my surroundings grim to say the least. No contact with friends and no-one to talk to. Well, I wasn't about to spark a conversation with a double child killer. Healthcare units are usually quiet places, but with Huntley boarded-off from the rest of the unit there was a deathly silence.

We all hear about prisoners being locked-up for 23 hours a day. Come on, I was locked-up for 24 hours each day with this creature. 'Not even an animal, he's the Devil himself,' I told myself as I lay on my bed. Shit, it freaked me out. Yes, I was a brute on the streets, but that was teenage gang life; this guy had done horrible things including burning his tiny victims' lifeless bodies. I needed to get out, I was in panic mode.

'Help me,' I screamed deep inside. I was so confused by the situation my mood swings picked-up pace, I rose to my feet and out of anger started to rip open my wounds from the previous night to feel the pain. As a female nurse watching from outside asked me to stop, I heard the beast itself speak, 'Please mate, please stop hurting yourself, I'll give you some tobacco if you stop.' Sounded like a kind man, 'What a pathetic attempt to fool the officers and me, what an evil bastard,' a voice told me.

I can still hear those words today. I put my hands to my ears. I'd feared bullies since my early childhood, and I'd begun to fear the Devil after one of my teenage friend's experiments with the occult scared me, and here I was with the Devil himself speaking to me. Though he was trying to come across as kind, his words were haunting me. 'Real devils don't just attack, they act nice and pull you in and that's what he's doing,' I thought. Even though I was weak and needed a smoke I didn't accept gifts from the Devil!

The situation was surreal, you hear about dreadful cases in the news and they are shocking, and maybe, unlike you, I've lived a disturbed life but this was a real headfuck even for me. Huntley murdered Holly Wells and Jessica Chapman, two innocent ten-year-olds, in Soham, Cambridgeshire. They'd just popped out to buy some sweets when they walked past his house and he invited them in. When they first went missing the police released photographs of the girls wearing Manchester United shirts. The search for them was one of the most reported in British criminal history and Huntley even appeared on Sky News talking of the shock to the community at their disappearance. Their bodies were found near the perimeter at RAF Lakenheath in Suffolk. Just hours later clothing was discovered in the grounds of Soham Village College and Huntley was arrested.

Those poor girls had been missing for nearly a fortnight. Huntley had set them alight in a bid to hide evidence. He was charged with the two murders and detained under the Mental Health Act at Rampton Special Hospital before a judge decided he was fit to stand trial. He was then transferred to Woodhill and it was my misfortune to be right next to him.

One night a screw from the young offender unit came over to watch me in the cage. Maybe he only volunteered so he could have a peep at Huntley. He was the talk of the prison, indeed of the country. Out of boredom I think, the screw asked me to sit closer to the bars so he didn't have to keep getting-up to see me, and out of equal boredom I agreed. He asked me where I was from. 'Souf London, Guv,' I replied and he then asked what football team I supported. 'Chelsea, Guv, I bleed blue.' He then sparked a conversation with Huntley, 'Who do you support?' 'Manchester United,' Huntley replied. My hypervigilance went into overdrive as I remembered once more that his two young victims had been wearing those shirts; it sent shivers down my spine.

That part of the healthcare unit will haunt me forever; I'll always remember it as a place that must have held thousands of extremely disturbed men. I could make up things and exaggerate but I'm telling it plain and simple, to some this situation might seem minor and Huntley only spoke to me s couple of times, but the experience affected me deeply. I liked to self-destruct and cause may-hem, this situation hurt me. I didn't deserve to be locked-up with this type of individual. I was an immature 18-year-old with mental-health issues and this was making things worse by the minute.

A few days later as my mind was about to spiral downwards, I was sent back to the young offender unit. I was told my friend Roger had been moved to another prison. I never saw him after that, I do hope he sorted his life out and isn't sitting in a cell somewhere reading this. An officer informed me that I was to be moved in a couple of days' time.

'Where am I going, Guv?' I asked and the screw replied, 'HM Young Offender Institution Aylesbury.' So I packed my bags once more and waited to be trans-ported to this prison for young adult offenders serving four years to life. 'The roughest of the roughest,' someone tried to scare me, 'packed full of the worst killers, rapists and thugs.' 'This is going to be fun,' I thought to myself as I set off to spend more than two years amongst them!

Mental Me

CHAPTER 2

The Horror of Aylesbury

One more step along the world I go, a few words I turned into a song, that I would sing at the top of my voice in police stations, court cells and prison vans. It gave me an overwhelming feeling of madness deep in my soul. It goes like this:

'One more step along the world I go,
From the old things to the new,
Keep me travelling along with you,
And it's from the old I travel to the new
Keep me travelling along with you …'

'Oh, what a lovely voice I have,' I told myself as the prison bus wound its way through the Buckinghamshire countryside. Once again, my situation would become disturbing, but this time round I'd lose the plot altogether. That's the scariest side of mental-illness, when you are unaware you're doing strange things. 'What did you just say about me?' 'Why's he looking at me?' 'They're going to kill me!' You get the idea don't you?

I was going to lose my mind completely, I'd not be in touch with reality, very funny, I know what you're thinking, that I was never in touch with reality in the first place, but I mean, errrmm, what other examples can I share with you. Put it this way, as an eleven-year-old I started to experiment with the odd bit of arson, petrol bombs, setting light to the grass. Well, I'd now got to the age where I was about to give it another go. 'I should have given it up back then as a child but when you're good at something why waste your talent?'

I'd categorise my two-and-a-bit years in Aylesbury as when I was 'lost in the system.' Once the sweat box passed through the outer gates we headed to the Induction Unit where I'd stay for the first month and be educated about the rules and procedures of the place which was a male young offender prison that normally only held long-termers.

As young offenders it's rare to be categorised, but if Aylesbury YOI was ever categorised it would have been as a Category A top security prison. This little hideaway held some really disturbed youngsters. As a matter of fact, it held the most dangerous young criminals in the country, serving sentences of from four years to life. The kind of cases that get media attention, notorious killers, rapists, thugs and paedophiles. If they were found guilty and aged between 18–21 you can bet your life on it they ended-up in this prison. Not a healthy option with those types believe me.

As I always seemed to have neighbours from hell it's not hard to figure out I was spoilt for choice in this place: Londoners, Mancs, Scousers, Geordies, this little gaff really did cater for the country's finest. There were Burger Bar Boys from Birmingham, one of that city's most notorious criminal outfits; also their arch rivals the Johnson Boys. There were some from the notorious Gucci Man Gang in Moss Side, Manchester and youngsters from South London, who'd go head-to-head settling scores in the education unit. To the screws, who mostly lived locally, it could be just a few stupid city boys trying to prove themselves, but in reality these 'little wars' had been going on for generations. From adults shooting each other over drugs to juveniles 30 deep on bicycles fighting each other in places like Brixton and Peckham.

After induction I was allocated to my wing where I was to settle and begin serving my time. Heading to a new wing was always daunting as you never knew what lay ahead. Would I have enemies? Who would be next door to me? In fact, my first next door neighbour turned out to be your average guy, just in for 16 years for a handful of kilos of heroin. Did I mention that his father and uncles were members of the Turkish Mafia, oh yeah, the type that torture and kill people for fun. But if you're picturing this big mafia-type guy, strong and bold then you're wrong. Mo was a right wimp; a nice guy though. Put it this way he was just a little runner for the elders in his family.

Little I say, he would tell me stories of how he'd drive carloads of heroin from place-to-place; I'm talking two hundred grand's worth, as if he was doing a paper round. As we sat in the corners of our cells and spoke to each other through the wall he told me stories of people being tortured over drug deals and held in freezers in dodgy kebab houses. I won't bother telling you about what they used to do to the kebab meat, work it out for yourself.

Mo once swallowed two AA Duracell batteries and was rushed to Stoke Mandeville Hospital before he started to be poisoned by the mercury; they cut his stomach open and removed them. This wasn't the first act of self-harm I'd witness. When you throw the country's most disturbed teenagers together it's a recipe for disaster. Just witnessing some of the gruesome acts was enough to leave you with PTSD and that was just the self-harm. Mo survived that episode with just a scar to show for it. The poor guy had a visit from his family and cried to them over his long sentence. They just slapped him and told him to be a man. I bet he wished he'd taken a different job as a kebab delivery boy on a moped.

I started to learn how things worked pretty quickly. To talk with each other we'd speak through the walls, but to talk to my upstairs neighbour I'd drain out my toilet and he would too, then we'd speak through the bowl. Imagine walking in and seeing your partner with their head down the toilet bowl! If I wanted to pass my neighbour something I'd make a line. I'd do this with a piece of string, put something on the end to weigh it down, and my neighbour would hold a newspaper out of his window. I'd swing the line in his direction until it hooked around the newspaper, then tie anything we wanted to exchange to it and let him reel it in.

If a neighbour two floors up and five cells along wanted to pass me something he'd unroll some toilet paper and let the breeze blow it in my direction until I could grab it and then I could pull in anything I wanted. The only thing was that this type of line passed many cells and if I was being sent a packet of biscuits some hungry little thief might steal them before they reached me.

If you wanted to open a tin of tuna you'd simply stab the top a few times with a biro, to make a big enough hole to hook your tap into, then rip the lid off. You could then enjoy your John West and keep the lid as a weapon. If you wanted to boil water, you could adapt your radio lead by sticking two paper clips into the holes at the end of it. Then carefully poke them into a bowl of water, switch on, and if the whole unit's electricity didn't blow you were on your way to a nice warm cup of Rosy Lee.

I managed to get a job as a landing cleaner. The money wasn't too bad for a full-time job, six quid a week. 'Good money for a nutcase,' I thought. I started a bit of tobacco dealing. The rules were simple, I give you half an ounce and you give me back an ounce on canteen day (that's when purchases like cigarettes and sweets are delivered to inmates once a week). I'd get 'burn cats' at my door offering me their life savings for one roll-up, come canteen day my cell looked like a corner shop. The only bad thing was that if you were caught tobacco dealing you'd be placed on the anti-bullying unit. In the end, I gave it up, but it was hard as I was used to getting all those little goodies.

I moved-up from cleaner to servery worker, meaning I cleaned the servery and handed out food to other inmates; the bonus was that all the leftover food me and the other workers got to share. A fair number of 'poncey' screws would steal food for themselves, I hated it when they did that. They had money and a home to go to and they took the prisoners' food. I remember when they made us serve pork sausages to Muslim inmates pretending they were halal beef.

There was just one decent officer on this wing called Bob Stevens. Let me tell you something, this man was like my guardian angel during my time on that unit. I swear I'm getting quite emotional as I write this because if it wasn't for Mr Stevens I'd be dead or locked-up in some mental facility and that's from my heart. He is someone that I'll always remember and respect.

I must also introduce you to someone else who was to impact greatly on my life, but this time in a wholly negative way that caused me to enter the darkest mental battle of my life. He was a fellow prisoner called Wayne Lister and the effect he was to have on my mental wellbeing is as you will see a recurring theme of this book. I haven't shared this story with many people, so think yourself lucky. Also think yourself lucky you've never been through something like this.

I was by now settled on my prison wing. I was a trusted prisoner and if I'd carried on like that I'd probably, eventually, have been granted parole. But all that was about to change and due to a disturbing incident I nearly didn't go home at all. I've been happy to write about my time inside so far, but this was always going to be a touchy subject. Though I've nothing to fear nowadays so here goes.

Cleaning the servery one afternoon I spotted a new inmate waiting by reception with his belongings. My hypervigilance from years of being in gangs and facing danger meant I was always scanning for threats. My PTSD was still undiagnosed at the time but one of the main symptoms, at least in my case, is hypervigilance. I'd check everything out: people, places, smells, noises. I was constantly in survival mode because with PTSD your mind believes you are in danger. The level may not always be high, you may be relaxed at times, but once hypervigilance kicks in your alertness is something else. Sometimes you're correct, yes you are in danger, and you need to run or fight. But sometimes you're wrong. It can become extremely tiring trying to work things out. So, looking on at the new prisoner he seemed to be a well-liked guy as other inmates were talking to him. This alerted me, 'Why's he so popular?' and 'Why's he so friendly?' If it was a new prisoner that no-one paid attention to, who sort of faded into the background, my alertness wouldn't have done overtime.

It wasn't long, around a week or so, that we started to chat, and I soon learned I was right to be alert around this new guy. Wayne Lister was serving life for murder and attempted murder. During the late hours one night two students were walking home across one of the bridges over the River Thames after a night out with friends. As they did so three adults were walking in their direction and as they came face-to-face these adults started to attack and rob the them.

By coincidence a second random group of adults was heading in the direction of this attack. The students asked this second group for help, but instead of doing so they joined in the attack. As it became more violent the robbery turned to murder. The attackers picked-up the two by now unconscious students and threw them off the bridge into the fast flowing water below.

One student was lucky. He was kept afloat by his rucksack and woke to find himself floating past Big Ben. Half-an-hour later, in shock, confused and suffering from hypothermia, he was rescued. The other student never regained consciousness and the river washed up his body later. Wayne Lister was 17 at the time. He was sentenced to life for murder and attempted murder along with another 17-year-old and his girlfriend. Each of the other three adults were also sentenced to life with long minimum tariffs, i.e. time to serve.

Once I knew of Lister's background, I kept a close eye on him. He began to try to make jokes with me about one thing or another and I didn't like them. Back then my alertness and anxiety made me a sensitive person and I couldn't take a wind-up too well. 'He's taking the piss,' I thought to myself but carried on as normal and pretended to laugh with him. Then one night on association I learned of his violent side. As I got stuck into a game of pool Lister sat down opposite and started to call me a 'prankster.' I turned to him and said, 'Don't take the piss, Bruv.' In a flash he responded by jumping-up and screaming, 'What the fuck!' He then head-butted me, and catching my bottom teeth my brain was rattled and I fell to the floor, only to jump up with the pool cue. I screamed in true fighting talk, 'Come on then!' I noticed his head pouring with blood from him head-butting me in the mouth.

By this time the alarm had been triggered and the screws got hold of Lister. I was taken to the end of the association room where all the lads were asking me what had happened. As I was telling them, Lister came running in trying to attack me again, but this time the screws dropped him to the floor and took him to the punishment block. He was given two weeks in there.

I sat in my cell and wondered if this killer was to be brought back onto the unit. I began to worry about him returning, so I asked an officer and was told he was indeed coming back. At night I couldn't get him out of my mind, I wasn't in control of the situation. Being locked-up on my own with just worrying thoughts, they became obsessive. I was thinking, 'Fuck, this guy is going to kill me now.' I thought of the situation twenty-four-seven, and for those two weeks I hardly slept as I let the anxiety take over my mind. I was convinced that he'd nothing to lose and was now going to kill me.

Soon the time came for Lister's return. I was serving up the daily shit on a tray and noticed him in the queue. His eyes met mine and I saw him looking at me with pure hatred. Those eyes were dark, just like mine when I became psychotic. I never knew as I looked at them how long that moment would stay in my head and replay over-and-over causing me to have mood swings at the drop of a hat. I didn't know that the incident would give me flashbacks and PTSD for the next 15 years or more.

Lister's extremely uncomfortable stare only added to my fears that he was now after me. I was going to have to be on alert as we lived in this little box of a wing together and he could attack me at any time. I learned of an attack he'd had done with a plastic knife on another inmate. I began to lose the plot. Soon me and Lister were talking again, and we shook hands, but I was trusting no killer, in my eyes it was a front for him to kill me when I least expected it.

My paranoid thoughts went out of control. When my servery duties finished, I'd clean the landings, the only thing was that Lister cleaned the grounds outside, so we came into contact if only occasionally. These were anxious moments as it was just the two of us on a corridor. My mind had been completely taken over with the thought of him planning to kill me. I was living in flight mode. I believed I was going to be killed but I'd no-one to tell and nowhere to run.

My sleep became unbearable with nightmares of Lister stabbing me to death and dying alone in this hell-hole. If people were shouting from the windows, I'd have to keep an ear out in case they were talking about me. If I was watching the news and the weather forecast came on and I heard the word rain I would mishear 'Wayne' and it would send a shiver down my spine and cause a panic attack. Anything that reminded me of him scared the shit out of me. However, I'd heard rumours that he was moving to an adult prison and gave a sigh of relief, but something told me, 'Listen mate this is just the start.'

The day came when he was going to be moved, but the damage was done. He'd never got to kill me like he did that student but maybe he would send others to do that. By now I was completely paranoid; the officers noticed my intense mood swings and one day whilst out cleaning one of my friends was keeping his distance. I asked him, 'What's the problem?' and he told me I was becoming aggressive and switching mood all the time. It was the first time I'd any sense that I was changing, but the confusing thoughts and feelings were difficult to work out.

I took out my frustration on a friend from Norwich called Billy Ward. I was winding him up, but all of the time the niggling and intrusive thoughts of Lister were coming to get me, making me tease Billy, take out some of what I was going through on him. I lost it and threw a bottle of cleaning liquid at his head and I then attacked him. I lost my job and I lost the plot let me tell you. So now without a job I'd lie on my bed thinking, thinking, thinking. I just couldn't stop my thoughts spinning and I was becoming more and more obsessed with images of other prisoners killing me.

I can feel mental health disorders coming on, can you? Lister was gone from view but his scent was still present, he remained there haunting me. Dear reader, I give you one severe, obsessive-compulsive disorder!

One, Two, Three, Four, Five … One, Two, Three …

A s I write this, I'm listening to Katie Melua singing 'Closest Thing to Crazy.' Back in those messed-up years I'd sit in my cell listening to this song and I was indeed *crazy*. Wayne Lister was long gone in physical form, but he was still there attacking me mentally. The paranoia overwhelmed me. I'd remember his cell number, No. 217. Nearly 20 years later I still see those numbers, or a mix of them and it triggers flashbacks. One of my local buses is the 127 which is a mix of those numbers, so can you imagine dealing with PTSD triggers when trying to do normal, everyday things. I might go for a walk with my family, they are calm and normal, then I see that bus go by and the numbers remind me of prison incidents. I start getting agitated. I want to leave and leave quickly. My family don't understand, I mean in those early years even I didn't understand why I'd end up snapping or arguing with them. I was seen as a 'nutter' or 'horrible' but in fact I was traumatised by something that gave me flashbacks and mood swings.

When people lose control of their feelings and daily life, they can become obsessed with things to try to regain some sort of control. So, then comes an obsessive-compulsive disorder. I remember Lister was always fifth in the dinner queue, something my hypervigilance picked-up on whenever I heard the number five or even other numbers. Whatever I might associated him with would haunt me. I started to tap things five times, my mind would say, 'If you don't tap that wall five times you're going to die,' and I'd do it. If I wanted to watch 'Home and Away' I couldn't as it was on Channel 5. I started to do odd things, like hiding one of the balls when playing pool because it had a certain number on it I didn't like. If I didn't hide the ball I'd die. Come on, I know it's weird but if you thought you were going to get killed you'd hide the ball too.

If I saw a mate, I'd try to shake his hand five times, by the third time he would be getting pissed-off, by the fifth we would be fighting and I'd be thinking, 'Fuck, I've just shook his hand, fuck, what if he shook Wayne Lister's hand when he was here.' I'd then go and scrub my hands but hold on a minute Lister must have touched most of the things on this prison wing at some time or other, I'd better wash my hands constantly and that's what I did. Each time there was a reminder, there was a reaction in my body, that of fear, and panic in my chest.

Every little thing in my cell was immaculate, if anything was untidy it would affect me, if there was a dirty mark on the wall then I couldn't look towards it. I was in a constant state of fear, aware of every breath, every thought running through my head, if a hair on my arm moved, I was immediately aware of it. 'Shit I forgot to touch that cupboard five times earlier, I better do it now.' This went on twenty-four-seven, it was complete mental torture. I'd switch on the TV or the light five times. 'But did I only count to four? Fuck I better do it again.'

As I lay there, I could hear talking out of the window. I got up and listened, 'Yeah, I'm gonna plant a left hook on that Paki Rollins.' They were going to attack me. But that person might just have just said to his mate, 'Yeah I just read a good book by Jackie Collins.' Yet I was convinced I was going to be attacked, I'd lose it and smash my cell to pieces, kick hell out of the door, thinking, 'Come on then, kill me.' I was a complete nutter, it was horrible, and it was a bad, bad time for me.

'Rollins pack your things you're moving upstairs,' ordered the screw. Shit what if Wayne Lister has been in that new cell before. I really didn't want to move. I was barely keeping control of the current cell what with the compulsive cleaning and obsessive counting. Thirty minutes later I was in my new bedroom, I lay there haunted at the thought that Lister might have been in there. I started to wash my hands over-and-over again. The hours passed and after doing this and tapping things hundreds of times I finally lay down on the bed.

Now, as I was a graffiti writer in my younger days I had the instinct to notice writing or graffiti, whether it was in pen, faded or fresh, old scratches, I'd notice it. I lay there with a thousand thoughts running through my head when I noticed some tiny writing on the back of the door. I stood up and walked towards it.

Fuck me, my heart began to beat rapidly, was this a horror movie or what; it read 'Lister woz 'ere.' I nearly fainted with fear, 'Shit he's been in here; I'm trapped with him all over this cell. Shall I press the alarm and tell the screws?' But I wasn't a grass. Even though it wasn't grassing just me being mental. Can you imagine, 'Guv, guv help I'm stuck in this cell with Wayne Lister.' The officer would probably say, 'Rollins, Lister left this prison three months ago.' He would then get straight on the phone to the psychiatrist.

I went to sit on the bed but jumped back up, I couldn't even sleep in it, it would be like sleeping with the Devil. I grabbed my blanket and curled up on the cold prison floor. The night officer looked through the flap and saw me, concerned he asked what I was doing, and I just told him the bed was uncomfortable. He must have wondered why I thought a cold prison floor was so comfy. But my mental health was in a state of disaster. When any new inmates came onto the wing they were like new Wayne Listers, I was convinced they were going to kill me. Still haunted by Lister I noticed another guy I was paranoid about pull out a blade and place it back in his waist band. I was right he *was* going to stab me. But if he'd wanted to do so he'd have done it there and then, and he had no reason to want to harm me. But I didn't see it that way at all.

Through these paranoid times Mr Stevens who I mentioned earlier kept me alive with his kindness and wind-up jokes, if it wasn't for that I'd surely have killed myself. He once went to the screws' canteen and brought me a bacon roll, the nicest roll I ever ate in my life, because Aylesbury food was rotten but mostly because it was an act of kindness, something I rarely saw in that environment. There were no nice vibes, just constant threats. Mr Stevens would give me tobacco when I was going off my head, that man saved me and I can't thank him enough. He'd worked in the prison system for years and once told me in all that time he only ever cared about me and one other prisoner. That there alone kept me alive as it made me feel like I was a human being.

With all this paranoia going on in my head, the prison wing still ran like normal. None of my friends realised the problems I was wrestling with inside my head. They knew I'd the potential to flip out, but can you blame them? They too had the potential to flip, we were all nutters, most of my friends were killers, but that was just Aylesbury for you. If you went in there a 'scar virgin' I'm sure you'd leave mentally scarred.

The horrors of Aylesbury have had a long and lasting effect. I'll give you a brief idea of some of the prisoners I was locked-up with and although we may have 'got along' affected my state of mind badly at times. First off, Fergus Tracy. He was a nice little guy but an awful self-harmer, just thinking of what he used to do makes my stomach churn. He'd slice his wrist, stick his fingers in the wound and pull on his ligaments so he was waving them at you. His arms looked deformed where he'd cut so much.

The thing about being a self-harmer in jail is you don't seem to care about the scars, because you have years to do and freedom is a distant dream, also it's the norm to see people with slashes all over their body. You're not thinking about meeting the woman of your dreams and having to explain the scars up from your wrists. It would be a red flag to a woman to stay away from you as you obviously have problems you might not have dealt with. Or maybe years later going on holiday, people looking at your scars glistening in the sun. It's not normal; you would feel like a freak from the stares you got.

Tracy's neighbour, a psychopath, had much neater, littler razor slices covering his whole body, I mean from the neck downwards. One day I asked the neighbour what he was in prison for. He replied without showing any emotion that he'd beaten a man to death with a brick. His reason why? He felt like it. That type of answer was the norm in Aylesbury. It was a sick, sick place, so many of the prisoners were mentally challenged; I'm surprised there were only two suicides whilst I was there, over the two years. Suicide in prison is a dark thing, who would want to die in that place. Although it crossed my mind, I never wanted my soul stuck there forever.

There was a group of prisoners trained to 'listen' to other prisoners' problems and perhaps unsurprisingly they were called 'Listeners.' They wore white T-shirts with a badge, they were there to prevent suicides. I never spoke to any of them as I found it awkward telling others about my problems and I was highly suspicious of anything like this. But I'm sure they helped many vulnerable prisoners. There were also charities that sent people to visit prisoners who had no-one on the outside. I remember an inmate getting quite happy that he had a visitor coming at the weekend, even though it was a charity worker and a stranger. I felt I was lucky having people out there who wanted to visit me, write to me and send me money. Some prisoners had nothing, and I think that made them more likely to harm themselves. Fergus Tracy was one of those.

Fergus' crime wasn't any more pleasant than those of the other killers walking around. He attacked a merchant seaman in a churchyard and the police suspected it was a homophobic offence and Tracy himself told me he killed him because he was gay. This aside Tracey was my mate and would always run to me if he had problems with other inmates. A killer running to me for help, a crazy thought. He was extremely disturbed and would drink window cleaner to prove he was mad, but we already knew he was. He gave up in the end and was found hanging in Belmarsh Prison.

My next 'buddy' was not your average killer. He told me he was deeply ashamed of and affected by what he'd done. Cooky was a Geordie addicted to heroin on the out. We would sit up all night talking by the pipes about life and whatever. Just never mention fish and chips around him. One day he and his girlfriend were out trying to make quick change to score some heroin. Remember what I already told you heroin does to the human mind; Cooky was a good kid before he got addicted to it. And a good kid now he was off it. He and his girlfriend spotted an old lady walking through their estate and Cooky decided to snatch her bag. The girl waited around the corner while Cooky ran up to the woman and grabbed the bag, she fell to the floor and Cooky legged it. They opened the bag to find only a parcel of fish and chips. Tragically, two weeks later the old lady died of a blood clot in her leg; Cooky got caught, went to prison and never heard from his girl again. He was a skaghead bag-snatcher but was also human and killing himself over his actions. I became his shoulder to cry on.

Another prisoner I'd chat to was Benny Williams who drowned an elderly vicar in a bathtub before dismembering his body. The victim's severed head and some of his remains were found in a bag behind a leisure centre on the South coast, his torso by the side of a main road. Benny told me he'd planned to dump the torso out at sea and that his reasons for killing the man were because he'd sexually abused him when he was an altar boy. He was a quiet inmate that kept himself to himself. They always say be wary of the quiet ones. Years later he won the right to appeal against his murder conviction and a retrial was ordered. He was acquitted; throughout the trial he kept stressing the abuse and somehow walked free. On his release he made up a hit list of men that he planned to kill, claiming he wanted to rid the world of paedophiles. After a trail of horrors that I won't burden you with he was convicted of a new murder and sentenced to life. He now identifies as a woman having performed a DIY sex change in his cell, cutting off his testicles and slicing his penis shaft in half. Just one of many prisoners that I spent time with and see popping-up in the news now and then. It was one fucked-up hell-hole and I'll tell you that for nothing.

Let's get back to my own violent instincts for a while. If a new boy entered the unit and I was convinced he was after me, I'd think about it twenty-four-seven. These times were awful; I was scared stiff, having panic attacks, constantly biting my nails, even dancing on top of the sink. I was off my nut, but I'd put a mask on, stand with a knife and fork, trance music pumping from my stereo, and I'd go mental, waving cutlery around as I danced the night away. If the screws came to my door flap I'd scream at them. Everyone thought I was crazy, but I was raving mad.

These potential new threats would take over my mind and attack me mentally, so I came up with the perfect plan. I'd attack them first. Fuck me what a genius idea, you know what, I'm quitting writing this book to become a rocket scientist. So, who wants to be my first victim hey, come on who wants it? Clarkey was a huge loudmouth who no-one liked. Whilst trying to catch a bit of a nap after a night of raving, somebody started to slam my flap waking me up. I looked up and Clarkey was there, he called me a prick, so I told him to fuck off.

The next day I was having a nap and it happened again, bang, bang, bang. I looked-up and he was staring at me through the flap. He simply said to me, 'What?' This was a horrible thing about prison and can add to paranoia. The cell doors have a flap that a screw can open to check on you. But prisoners can do this too, so you could be lying there, and any stranger might open the flap and just stare at you. This would make you alert and ready to fight. I told Clarkey I was going to kill him and off he went. I walked down to the servery where he was handing out the yoghurts and he threw mine at me. I went mental and lunged at him. The screws got to me and escorted me to my cell.

I never liked Clarkey. There were rumours that he was in prison for rape, but no-one had any proof. That's the thing in prison you could think someone was a good guy and be friendly with them but in fact they could be a rapist or paedophile. I remember working as a cleaner with one guy and we became friendly, playing pool together and sharing tobacco when either one of us had run out. I had photos of my niece I showed to him like a proud uncle, he didn't take too much notice of them but a few months after he left I found out he was a paedophile. They were certainly amongst us, but I never heard of the rape of another inmate. I think the old film 'Scum' starring Ray Winston gave out that impression, but I never witnessed it.

Prisoners might have been attacked for being gay in young offender institutions in my day. Things were different in adult prisons though; gay relationships went on, but they were kept hidden. British prisons, though brutal at times, didn't so far as I can tell carry the worry of rape, not like in USA prisons where I'm told rape is a standard thing, which is disturbing in itself. One disturbing sexual incident did happen in Aylesbury when a rapist grabbed a female officer in an education room. Of course, he didn't get far with the officer pressing her alarm. That prisoner must have fallen down a few flights of stairs 'by accident' on the way to the segregation unit! It was the talk of the prison at the time. We never saw the officer or the inmate again.

The hatred inside of me for rapists grew stronger and after some beefs with Clarkey and believing that he was a rapist I sat in my cell agitated. Like Wayne Lister he was 'with me,' in my mind attacking me. Right 'I'm going to hurt him,' I thought. I made a knife out of what I could find but this sad bastard was so big I wouldn't be able to get to him properly. So, I filled a sock with old batteries and come association I was shaking with rage to use it. The screw asked if I'd calmed down and I swore I had, I walked into the association room and saw Clarkey playing pool. I waited a moment then pulled out my weapon and set about him, whacking him over the head until he snapped a pool cue around my jaw. 'Fuck that hurt,' I gasped as the screws wasted no time dropping me and whisking me to the punishment block.

The segregation unit is grim, cold and very lonely, a shit hole. You're allowed out for half-an-hour a day, and that is only into another grimy little box outside to walk about on your own. The seg screws are the worst of the worst, they treat you like dirt. I think they are near enough all of them sadistic bastards, who I'm convinced spit in your food and definitely talk to you like you are less than human. I was sentenced to three weeks in there, three weeks of talking to no-one was going to be hard.

I'd managed to smuggle some tobacco into the seg but had no matches, so I banged on my neighbour's wall. 'Oi, Bruv, any matches?' A conversation started and we exchanged tobacco and stories. The other prisoner was in for robbing a Chinese takeaway. The report indicated that he'd committed an horrific murder and when I heard this the Aylesbury ghosts started to come back and haunt me again in the form of PTSD.

CHAPTER 4

Violent Young Offenders

I don't suppose you lot know the feeling of punching and kicking a wet, naked body. Well, I hope you don't, you disturbed so and so's. To be honest you know by now my life has been rife with violence; that which I've been dealt and that which has been dished out to me. The number of punches I've thrown and received is high. But punching and kicking the wet naked body of a paedophile did feel pretty good, and to be honest he was extremely lucky I hadn't experienced fatherhood at that point of my life, or I'd probably have hurt him a lot more.

Around this time, I'd resumed cleaning and I must admit my cleaning was pretty good. Thanks of course to my obsessive-compulsive disorder. 'Listen Rollins, if you don't clean that landing ten times you're going to die' my mind was telling me. We'd had a special guest just moved onto the prison wing. ''Allo, 'allo, 'allo, Jake Jennings.' Jennings was dubbed a 'teenage paedophile' by the media. He was being held in a strip cell, which had no windows so he couldn't be verbally abused by other inmates. He wasn't allowed to socialise with the normal inmates as he would have been attacked within minutes. The whole unit was talking about who would catch him first and I told them that I was up for it, the only thing was how were we ever going to get our hands on the guy?

Jennings was in fact a nasty piece of work, this 19-year-old trainee banker was and will always be a real threat to children. Surfing internet chat rooms he'd prey on young girls. One day he logged into a paedophile site and kept demanding that he wanted to 'buy' a young girl. Silly Jennings didn't realise this site was fake and had been set up by the Met with the help of the FBI in a bid to catch predators like him. Undercover officers agreed to sell Jennings a nine-year-old girl. He told one of them, 'I'm not going to mistreat her, not too much, if you know what I mean.'

The officers met him at London's Victoria Station and took him in a cab equipped with video recording equipment to a hotel where he was arrested. He had an imitation firearm in his waistband, a teddy bear and a condom. When police raided his home they found a lot of disturbing items in his safe: leg shackles, handcuffs, an extending police baton, a knife and a roll of duck-tape. They also found newspaper cuttings of notorious child exploitation cases.

One week after he was caught Jennings had been due to start helping out as a volunteer at a children's centre and it was by stroke of luck that the police caught him in time. He pleaded guilty to attempting to incite another to procure a child under 16 and possessing an imitation firearm. He was sentenced to three years in prison and that's how my knuckles came to make contact with him.

The talk on the prison wing was that Jennings was a dead man walking, but no-one could get their hands on him. One day whilst the wing was on lock-down me and a couple of mates were out cleaning the landings. As I tackled the second floor one of them came running up the stairs and informed me that Jennings was alone in the showers. I said I'd meet him in there in a minute, quickly looked to see if any screws were about and discovered the coast was clear. I opened the shower room door and was met by the sight of the others kicking the shit out of a naked Jennings.

I ran over and started to attack him, it was a weird feeling punching bare wet skin as I aimed my fists at his back and ribs. Each time they would slide off. We started to kick him all over the place and you could say we left him in a bit of a mess to say the least, we should have brought our cleaning equipment and dealt with it but instead we ran off and got stuck into cleaning back on the landings. My heart was pounding as the adrenalin rush was near finishing and that is when I heard a commotion downstairs.

'ROLLINS… THE THREE OF YOU… GET TO YOUR CELLS… RIGHT NOW!' The screw's face was bright red, we were in trouble now. I walked past him, saying nothing and went into my cell where I was banged-up. But come on all you wonderful readers my street name wasn't Sevens for nothing, ever heard of the term 'lucky seven.' My door opened and the red-faced screw had something to say. 'Sorry Rollins, Jennings said you never did anything, you can come out and clean the showers.' The other two each spent a long time in the punishment block for that attack and got extra months added to already long sentences. They were held up as heroes for a while in Aylesbury, while I had to calmly smile to myself. I can't deny that at that stage in my life it was a proud moment, but please understand I was an extremely disturbed individual at the time.

Jake Jennings was eventually released from Aylesbury into a high-security probation hostel where there were strict rules, such as no pornography. Nearly straightaway he was caught with hardcore pornographic material in his room and this raised concerns about him reoffending. A police spokesperson said, 'Jennings isn't safe to be back on the streets for years. He had all the implements to kidnap torture and possibly kill a child.' He was right, nearly eleven years later having changed his name, within the space of a week he tried to kidnap a ten-year-old girl and a five-year-old in separate incidents. He was spotted by an off-duty police officer who shouted at him causing him to flee. After trying to snatch another young child he was caught nearby and again they found shocking items in his possession. He was sentenced life in prison. I don't think offenders like him are ever safe to have in society.

Around this time, I really started to become institutionalised. Not having much contact with the outside world can have a major toll on mental health. It got to the point where I was so paranoid that I couldn't face leaving the unit, so I hardly breathed any fresh air at all. I started to cut-off all family visits as I couldn't bear to see them after my mother, my brother-in-law, my sister and my sister's newly born baby visited me. I couldn't cope with it anymore, what with the noise and number of people in the visits hall. I was so anxious I was frozen in fear. They walked over to the table and I couldn't even stand up to hug them. I was in a hypervigilant state, alert to every noise around me, from someone crunching on a crisp to someone passing by and the mass of conversations. If I stood up to hug them I felt I might collapse from the anxiety. I decided to have no more visits.

I went back to my cell and thought about how their lives had moved on. I'd become a total stranger to them, lost in the system. I started to cover my cell window so that I was in complete darkness. I spent weeks like that. And as I'd a tendency to self-destruct, I thoroughly enjoyed the pain I felt. The paranoia worsened and I was convinced half of the unit were out to get me.

One day I acted like a right cocky little so and so by sticking my nose in somebody else's beef. Two boys were arguing over a gambling debt, the one in the wrong wouldn't pay up; he was being a bad loser. The other guy didn't have the bottle to fight for his rights. As I sat there and listened, something inside of me made me shout out, 'Do you think you could ever mug me off?' The wrong-un had no reply, I thought nothing more of it. The next day whilst sweeping the unit he was hanging around near the office. All I saw in his eyes was Wayne Lister. I stared back and he blurted out, 'What you looking at dickhead' and with that I ran over to him and whacked my broom over his head. The alarm went off and before I knew it I was locked-up in the punishment block again. It was a destructive way of coping, but by attacking him first and seeing the fear in him I didn't sit there with him in my head terrorising me. I'd won that battle so it didn't bother me, but I still had Lister in my head to torment me.

I know I brought this situation on myself, I butted into a guy's business when it had nothing to do with me, now I'd lost my job for the second time, but I was satisfied I'd found some sort of coping mechanism even if it was through violence. It had got to the point where I'd just attack another inmate without thinking at all. There are so many prisoners like this, but they don't know why they are acting that way and neither do the officers. I was out of control and the prison officers were starting to realise that something was wrong with me.

There was a meeting about my behaviour; concerns raised about my unpredictable outbursts of violence. Unknown to me there were discussions going on about my mental health and sectioning me was one option. But that would not have been a good idea while well into a prison sentence because my time inside would have been put on hold and I'd have been placed in a mental facility for any amount of time, and upon release I'd have gone straight back to prison. But what they had witnessed so far was nothing compared to the insanity I was soon to provide them with. Back on the prison unit without a job I lay in darkness with my paranoia doing overtime.

I bumped into the guy who'd been in the wrong and his eyes showed pure fear. He was a 'begging friend' in street terms, trying to be nice to me as he feared I'd attack him. I'd turned the tables; it was like I was Wayne Lister coming back from the segregation unit and the other boy was me living in fear of being hurt. I started to stay in my cell 24-hours a day in darkness; I didn't come out for association to make phone calls or even to shower. I began to stink, I reckon I didn't wash for weeks. And I'm not embarrassed to say that as I wasn't well. Have you ever come across someone that smelt bad and was in his own world mumbling things, the type of bloke that might make you want to cross over the road? Well that was me. I didn't care if I smelt though; mental folks don't seem to care about things like that. I cared about getting stabbed to death in the showers and that's what I believed was going to happen to me. My only escape from this living hell was to write poetry, and yes, those poems were depressing, mental and negative, all 600 of them. Yes, I wrote that many over my years in prison, had quite a few published. Some days I could write several, it was therapeutic, my only release from the craziness within.

Boy I'd come a long way from being strangled at my childminders as a five-year-old. Funny how things turn out, one minute you're normal, next being strangled, next writing your name all over London as a graffiti tagger and then mixing with the country's worst killers, oh mate was I living the life of Riley? You may have gone to university. I went to prison (okay a university of crime). Do you ever look back on your photo album and wipe off the dust saying, 'Oh look, there's Frankie, he was the life and soul of the party' or 'I've found a photo of Samantha, she was my closest mate back then.' I look at my album and it just has newspaper clippings of some of my mates from inside. Like I say, it's strange how things turn out...

CHAPTER 5

Fire Raiser

The screw informed me I was being moved off my unit onto a new one. For two reasons: it wasn't healthy, me rarely leaving my present unit for over a year; and because I was becoming 'unpredictable.' His words hit me like a nightmare come true.

'Rollins … a word please!

'Yeah Guv, what do you want?'

'You're moving.'

'Move off this unit, you must be nuts!'

Yes, I *was* nuts but there was no way I was going anywhere, 'I'd rather leave in a body bag,' I thought, 'I'm well and truly settled here.' The unit was my home, my safety, even though I never felt safe because I was overwhelmed with paranoia. But imagine being moved onto a new one altogether. It would be a whole new environment, a whole new place full of danger; a hundred new killers to watch my back for, more OCD to take care of.

I hadn't left my unit for a long time, nor breathed fresh air. I'd sit in my cell in pitch darkness for hours, days and weeks on end and now they wanted to throw me into a lion's den of uncertainty. 'Well fuck that mate, because I'M THE GOD OF HELLFIRE AND I BRING YOU FIRE.' I argued with the screw. I looked into his eyes, and they were smiling; he knew I was weak, he knew I couldn't do anything about it. But hold on a minute, 'I'M THE GOD … no hold on I've already said that.'

I walked back to my cell with my food. I sat down and really didn't feel like eating that shit on a tray. I started to panic, got out my pen and paper, and started a suicide note. 'Listen you dirty screws, I'll leave here in a body bag, watch.' I then posted this in the letter box when I was let out of my cell in the evening. I didn't even bother saying 'Bye' to my mother in the note, I was too crazy for that, I wasn't her son at that point, I wasn't anybody, just a freak or a fruitcake, mmmm fruitcake, I'm bloody well starving. I often felt I was starving in prison, to the point of eating toothpaste!

I was locked-up again in my cell for the night and that's when I lost it. I got together of all my magazines, clothes and sheets and threw them by the cell door. I picked-up my stereo and poems, wrapped them up and gently placed them in the corner of the cell. Well, come on, if I'd survived, I'd still want to listen to my music; music is the key to life remember. 'COME ON THEN, LETS FUCKING DO THIS.' I lit a roll-up, took a pull, then put the lighter to the magazines and things. Before you know it I was going up in smoke. I watched the fire burn like hell, if you'd looked into my eyes you would have seen the reflection of the red hot flames of hell because that's what Aylesbury was like. 'HERE WE GO, HERE WE GO, HERE WE GO.'

I ripped the TV from its cabinet and with all my strength smashed it off the ceiling. What a sound it made, that felt a lot better than crushing my toy cars under bus wheels as a small boy, this was proper destruction. I felt a bit like Lionel Richie for a minute 'dancing on the ceiling.' But hold on, no time to waste, I have to destroy myself too and with that I picked up the glass from the broken TV and started to slice my wrists.

The sound of the TV being smashed seemed to have got the screws' attention. I felt a bit sorry for the female screw who came to investigate, being met by the sight of flames and me screaming and bleeding. Panic alarms went off throughout the prison, screws rushed over to the unit to answer the alarm. They soon removed the plug in the door used to poke the fire hose through, in minutes the fire was out. I was then removed from my cell to be met by a handful of screws, nurses and firemen. I'm sure those firemen went home and it sparked a convo with the missus. 'Darling, how was your day? Mine was a bit hectic, got called out to that YOI, this right freak had set his cell on fire.' Well, listen firemen, I used to have a home too!

After I was taken from the cell I was rushed to the breathing apparatus, thinking back now, I really didn't care if I breathed again or not. My wounds were patched up and I was slung into a gated cell naked. As I lay there, I started singing my take on a Prodigy song 'I am the God of Hellfire.' That's when Mr

Stevens came to see me and slipped me some tobacco. That man kept me alive. I was in a right state, a state of disaster, this was normal though, this was my life, what a bloody life eh? I was serving a sentence for my crimes and at the same time I was paying the price mentally, maybe it was a life sentence when it came to the mental one. Would I ever be sane again, hold on a minute I know, yes I know. Was I ever sane?

I was put back in my old cell which stunk of burning and had been water-logged. First thing I always did whether in my home or back then in the cell was to switch on some music to liven-up the place. I stayed in that cage for a few days, and then was allocated back to the unit. I told the divvy screw I wasn't going nowhere. He was the one who'd found my suicide note, put it this way he wasn't a happy bunny. I looked for my stereo but couldn't find it, until I noticed it smashed to pieces under my bed.

Of course, I knew the divvy screw had done that to get to me and I started kicking the door until he appeared. I said 'I know what you've done to my stereo you mug,' but he replied, 'I don't know what you're going on about Rollins.' He then left smirking. Now remember I was the paranoid arsonist, who'd believe anything I had to say, so that screw carried on smirking every time he saw me.

There was talk of criminal charges being brought against me for arson, which carries a maximum sentence of life. But a decent screw told me to just say I was seriously intending to commit suicide, which I was anyway, so no charges were brought against me for the two fires.

Did I say two? Here we go again! A day later I'd been told to go to work as a prison dustman. I knew my nickname could easily have been 'Justin the Dustbin' so I refused preferring to sit in darkness. The next day I was taken to the punishment block for refusing an order. As I put on my trainers to head over there, I slipped a lighter and two pieces of glass in one of the soles. I was patted down on arrival, stuck in a grimy cell, and ten minutes later I was seated in front of the Governor.

'What's the problem Rollins?'

'I'm paranoid Governor.'

'We're all paranoid Rollins,' he replied as the other screws erupted in laughter.

If only those sad bastards knew how hard it was to tell somebody I was para-noid, and they just laughed. I was found guilty as always in the adjudication room and sentenced to three days in the punishment block. I think this was only because I'd started the fire on the wing as a bit of revenge in their eyes.

Back in the cell I was fuming. 'We're all paranoid Rollins … We're all paranoid Rollins,' I kept hearing those words and picturing them laughing at me. I hadn't been called Justin for ages, I wasn't human, I was just an animal in a cage, and they were the predators. I pulled out my lighter and the pieces of glass; the thing is there is nothing much in a punishment cell to burn. The only thing I could find was a toilet roll and a book, so I set them alight. The other thing is that punishment cells have no windows so within seconds the cell was thick with smoke. In a state I started to slice my wrists for the second time in a week. As the blood dripped to the floor, the smoke overwhelmed me, I couldn't breathe. The only 'fresh air' was full of smoke. I panicked and pressed the bell thinking, 'Fuck, I'm going to die this time, I'm going to die.'

I could hear the screw walking along the corridor and cried, 'Help Guv, help, help, help.' After looking in he shouted to the other screws that something was up, then he looked through the spy hole and grinned at me. The words another screw shouted out would haunt me for life. 'Is he bloody well hanging?' I felt that evil man was hoping I was dead. Now the first screw knew full well the fire had burnt out, all he had to do was let me out so that I could breathe. But, instead, he opened up the plug in the door and started to hose me down aiming the ice-cold water at my face which wasn't helping my breathing. The hose was so powerful it was pushing me up against the cell wall. I was crying inside as he grinned through the spy hole. Everywhere I ran in the cell he aimed it at me, I was drenched like a sewer rat, the cell was flooded out and I cowered down by the bed. The water stopped and the order was shouted out, 'Strip out of your clothes, now walk to the back of the cell, face the wall and put your hands on your head.'

The cell door opened. 'Don't fucking move, I'm going to place this riot shield against your back. Now walk backwards, hands on your stupid head boy, now step out of the cell.' After I did so I was pushed up against the wall by the screw with the shield; I was naked, couldn't breathe properly, was soaking wet, my hands were on my head and my arms were bleeding. I then had to slowly walk sideways with my nose pressed up against the landing wall to the next cell.

As I looked down to the bottom landing all I saw were eyes everywhere, screws, nurses and firemen staring at this animal. That moment was one of the lowest points of my life and, come on, I'd had quite a few but that is definitely one that has stayed with me. I was dubbed 'The Aylesbury Terrorist' after that; and every time a bunch of screws saw me they'd say 'Watch out here he comes, The Aylesbury Terrorist.' I was put on the breathing apparatus once again and was lucky I never died.

I always wanted to be crazy, now I bloody well was and it was a painful and lonely time for me. The prison bosses had had enough of me, I'd attacked a handful of other inmates, one with a weapon, set fires, flooded and smashed up prison cells. That only meant one thing: I should be sectioned under the Mental Health Act. I never knew the system was preparing for this to happen, but a decent nurse who liked me came to warn me about it. I was informed I was hanging by the skin of my teeth. I asked him where I'd be sent to, would it be Broadmoor? He told me there's a chance and that's all I needed to hear to calm down.

Broadmoor Special Hospital was hell on earth; it housed the most evil and insane people in the country. Serial killers, terrorists and cannibals. I'd a choice: carry on like I was and risk going there or calm the fuck down and just mix it with the average Joe-type killers. Did you know that Broadmoor puts on special discos for the patients there? What songs do you reckon? Louis Armstong's 'What a Wonderful World'? Dancing to 'Hey Macarena' with a cannibal? Or maybe Will Smith's 'Boom, boom, shake, shake the room tick, tick, tick, tick, boom' might work with a nail bomber? I chose Aylesbury, thanks.

I wasn't the only one losing the plot. Austin was a skinny little guy that would always ponce for tobacco. No-one had time for Austin, but I gave him a chance and would talk to him. He was pretty normal, but obviously had problems like the rest of us. I'd never watched somebody deteriorate mentally before until I watched Austin crumble. He would come to my cell and ask for my dog ends. I thought that was a bit dirty, but I let him have my ash tray to keep him happy.

Then one day he came to my cell and told me he'd found God and was really happy with himself. I was happy for him too; he was doing well for a few weeks. Then he started posting letters to me under my cell door. They were full of preaching and saying that I was his brother and so on for giving him dog ends. That it must have been the Christian in me. I started to notice he was acting a bit strange and stopped talking to him. He then informed me I was a sinner and that he didn't want to be around anyone as we were all evil.

Things started getting worse when he all of a sudden turned mute, didn't say a word to anyone for weeks. I realised he'd lost it when he appeared with rotten food on his tray from days before. Picture this, when Austin handed the servery lads his plate they would sit the fresh food on top of the rotten food, and his cup would have old tea bags in it. The guy was a right mess, and after seeing this for a few days I said, 'Clean your plate mate.' He informed me I was the Devil and he was going to stab me. I didn't take offence as this guy weighed just three-stone, he was so skinny if he turned sideways he disappeared. Then he flooded his cell and threw his live TV into the water. After that the screws brought in a psychiatrist.

It didn't take long before he snitched on a guy accusing him of being the anti-Christ and started threatening him. Austin was sectioned and never seen again. I did as the nurse said and got my head down, I didn't want to be following him to cuckoo land. Instead, I was put in touch with a criminal psychologist, called Rachel and after some hesitation started to speak to her about my issues. But by then I'd started fighting my mental issues on my own anyway.

One day when my OCD was telling me to touch this or touch that five times or something bad would happen, I just snapped and started screaming back at the voice, NO I WONT DO THAT, I DONT CARE, I'D RATHER DIE THAN CARRY ON LIKE THIS. That battle was so hard, when every other thought was saying, 'If you don't tap five times you are going to die.' I'd panic thinking, 'Did I touch that four or five times' and I'd have to do it again. But not anymore. I battled these thoughts constantly for a month or so; I mean sleepless nights, panic attacks and all sorts. Slowly the voice telling me to tap things or wash my hands started to fade. I was winning the battle, I still had the paranoia, but had conquered the OCD and was very proud of myself.

You know I loved to write my poetry and I also loved to read, so there was one thing I knew I always wanted to do and that was write a book. I started to write constantly over a few weeks and even though the standard was poor something good came out of it. It was the first time I made the painful discovery that I'd been living a lie. I wasn't proud of my race. I'd do things just to fit in and I was scared to show kindness in this brutal world. I was about to become close friends with a killer who switched something on inside of me that did make me proud of my race and that alone was one small but very important step on the road to recovery.

CHAPTER 6

The Colour of My Skin

For a few weeks during my time in prison I put pen to paper and wrote about my crazy life. But only when I was able to do this, as I'd started to get dizzy spells; I had to lie down every ten minutes because I thought I'd collapse. I was in-and-out seeing the prison doctors, but they never knew what the hell was wrong with me. Only now, when I look back, do I realise it was because I was questioning my background. The reason? I was lying to myself as I wrote about it.

Can you believe it that I was pretending I was white not, as I shall explain, of Sri Lankan heritage? I had panic attacks from fear that people wouldn't like me if I was not white like the rest of my family in Sutton. This stemmed from never knowing an Asian father and growing-up in a predominantly white town where there was a lot of racism and hatred. I grew-up with the white side of my family and believed I was also white like them, until the day came when I was to experience racism for myself. Being called 'Paki,' beaten and looked down upon affected me to the core. I hated it. Like most children I just wanted to fit in. But how do you fit in being brown within a white family in a racist environment?

After a few weeks of hiding my roots during my first attempt at writing about my life I gave up. It was too stressful, but I carried on questioning myself. I questioned why I'd tried to hide my race and buried other issues. Believe me it was painful not knowing my true origins. My problems with my identity were a big issue that alone had I think caused me to become a bad boy. How can you love a side of you when you were never taught to love that side? When all you've ever heard is Paki this and Paki that. I grew up in a place where Asians were bullied, where the National Front and Combat 18 (right wing and neo-Nazi groups) were often visible from their initials written on walls. But now I was digging away at my fears and that is why one day, when I heard there was a Sri Lankan boy on the unit, I decided to talk with him.

A youngster called Supenthar came to England hoping to help his family out of poverty and he was studying maths and science at what was Harrow College. He became friendly with four boys of Tamil descent when he needed protection due to being bullied by a Muslim gang. His Tamil acquaintances were all Hindu. The four of them took him to a restaurant in East London where they demanded money which they claimed he owed them. When he didn't settle this 'debt' they took him to a park where they attacked him, then beat him to death, dosed his body in petrol and set it alight. His charred remains were found the following day.

One of the Tamils was identified as their leader and was also being tried for another brutal murder. He'd killed a young man with an axe and chopped someone's hand off. This became one of the longest investigations at the time, costing millions of pounds in taxpayers money. He was found guilty of both murders, the others for that of Supenthar. All were sentenced to life in prison.

These cases were amongst the first to highlight Tamil gang violence in London, with the police starting-up a Tamil Taskforce, the equivalent to Operation Trident that targets gun crime in the capital. That is how I ended up meeting Nathan on my prison unit. I started to speak to him and we became friends. I know it sounds cheesy, but I was happy that I'd found a friend from Sri Lanka, like I'd discovered a little piece of me, no not the killer in me smart arse. Even though I believed at the time that my Sri Lankan roots were Sinhalese, he accepted me as his friend. I told him my father's family were Sinhalese and he had no problem with that, even though Sri Lanka had a history of bloody civil war between these groups. In fact, I later learned that my grandparents were Dutch Burghers, a small ethnic group in Sri Lanka, who were Roman Catholic (as I explain in the *Epilogue*).

After our friendship was struck, in no time I made friends with other Tamil boys and at that time they were like brothers to me. Forgetting for a moment their crimes, they had a gentle nature; they kept themselves to themselves and were peaceful in prison. Being with them made me feel good, I'd a sense of peace inside me for the first time in my life. I never once looked on Nathan as if he was a brutal killer; I looked at him as a friend and a brother. My days with him and my other 'brothers' only got better when we joined a cookery class together, those times were special to me. Put it this way they cooked the best Sri Lankan curry in the world, and for once I was proud to be a curry muncher. We would sit together away from other convicts and eat with our hands; those were some of the best days of my life back then.

I remember moaning to Nathan that I'd ages to serve. He quickly pointed out that he had to do a minimum of 16 years before he could even put up for parole. I quickly shut my mouth. He had a strong heart, but I don't know how he coped with that sentence on his head. When he and the other brothers held their Hindu festivals in the prison's Hall of Faiths they never forgot to bring me back some home cooked food, things which I'd never tasted before. That was a real treat after eating shit on a tray for so long. I even started to listen to a bit of Tamil music too; I'd lie there in my cell and feel at peace. I didn't have a clue what the guy was singing about, it could have been that I was a right wanker for all I knew, but I didn't care. I'd found just a little bit of peace in my life.

Things seemed to be brightening up for me, though don't let me lead you down the wrong road, I was still very unstable mentally, but I was starting to battle my anxious and paranoid thoughts. Rachel my psychologist who of course knew of my past behaviour was amazed at how I could be so popular on the prison unit with all this madness deep within my mind. It's weird looking back as she was truly impressed, but I was still very unwell. However, she was the professional and could see that I was different. She asked one day if there was anyone that I'd ever feared as a child or throughout my teenage years. I was too scared to answer the question, and it was swept away just like that.

Looking back, I can see what she was getting at. I was half-strangled by an older boy with fishing wire when I was five. That gave me PTSD, a fear and alertness of older, tougher boys, bully types. I attracted those types throughout my childhood, and always I had the same fear in my chest as the strangler gave me. All those years later my altercation with Wayne Lister had been like a volcano exploding. He was the real deal, a proper killer, and my breakdown began.

During my time in Aylesbury my father got in contact with me. 'Fuck me it must be Christmas,' I thought. Hold on, that wasn't a good phrase because he had never, ever contacted me at that time in previous years. I'd only seen him once since age two, and we'd shared one brief visit in HMP High Down when he randomly turned-up to see me. Aside from disrespecting my mother, claiming that he could have raised me better than her, the rest of that brief visit I hardly remember. But here he was again writing to me none the less and promising me all the stuff under the sun, a job fitting air conditioning and a roof over my head.

I was foolish and naïve to believe a man I always classed as spineless, that I grew-up hating, that brought me into the world but abandoned me. I never knew him, but I knew that I hated him. When a parent doesn't want to see you, protect you or fight your corner as a child you begin think you're not good enough. Worthless even. Especially if the other parent isn't reassuring you that you're valued and loved. You start to develop a core belief that you must somehow be bad as well. This leads to depression but can also make some of the most successful people. Many will try so hard to show their parents and the world that they *are* good enough, screaming out for praise, that they do extremely well at whatever they set out to be, but they may still have that deep belief that they are not good enough when alone.

One day whilst out of my cell on association I decided to phone Dad. I was a fighter but still vulnerable. I tried to ask him why he never bothered with me through my childhood and his response was, 'Son, you know I have my own family.' His words really made me feel good about myself, that's a laugh. I felt as good as a 'walking piece of shit' to be honest. It was just a reminder of how I wasn't worth anything, but that was nothing, wait until you hear this.

I was about to go up for parole, even though I'd more chance of winning the Euro Millions than getting it. None the less I tried for it, so I wrote to my father and asked him if he'd write me a reference about him giving me a full-time job, and yes you guessed it, he didn't even reply. So, I never got parole and when I got a copy of the parole report I realised why. Put it this way these are just a few things it said: 'Devil worshipper, known to use weapons, arsonist, self-harmer.' I can honestly say that there wasn't one good thing written about me, and the file was the size of a magazine. But they got it all wrong because I was the diamond in the dirt that hadn't been found, or maybe the loony in the dirt.

Out of anger and on impulse I wrote to my Dad telling him what I thought of him, I said he was a coward and the next thing I wanted to hear about him was that he was dead and said I wouldn't even attend the funeral. To top it off

I drew some graves with 'Dad' written on them, which although disturbing I still believe was quite creative, though I admit the funeral bit was a bit harsh. I could have done far better than that. It put the final nail in the coffin when it came to our relationship: he only phoned up the prison once he'd received the letter and demanded to speak to the Governor about punishing me. He'd more chance of speaking to Elvis Presley. Put it this way the Governor is the boss, all the screws underneath him or her look-up to that person even if they don't like them. Our Governor didn't answer young offenders' parents, this wasn't school, this was a brutal place and he had bigger fish to fry. He probably laughed at my father's request.

My cell door opened and I was told to go to the office. I arrived to see Mr Stevens, a senior officer, a nurse, and the chaplain (even though I'm not a Christian). The meeting was about my father's complaints. I politely told them that his and my business had nothing to do with them then walked out. I never heard about it again and the reason all those people were there was because they thought that I was going to be crazy again and start fires and so on. I washed my hands of my father after that. Grassing on his own son, couldn't even take my words on the chin, dear oh dear, hey! Damn! How a man can abandoned his child and then be angry that his child is pissed-off at him. If it had gone the wrong way and his complaints had been taken at all seriously I could have been taken down the punishment block!

I'll be honest. At times, my behaviour in prison sometimes got me what I wanted. Most screws don't give a toss about you. If you were to ask them for something, most of the time they'd accidently forget on purpose to get or do it. But my reputation as a nutcase got me what I wanted at times, which I used to my advantage whilst serving out my sentence. I was by now 20 and I'd been convicted at the age of 17 for the offence I was inside for. I was coming up to my release date, I'd spent three years in prison. Had I learned anything? Was I a reformed character, come on? All prison did for me was leave me even more fucked-up, in fact it left me with a lifetime of PTSD. Yeah, I learned to be more violent, more distant, and more alienated from normal society.

Three years before whilst on the street I'd be drunk half the time, then I was violent, now I was even worse. I went away a violent but vulnerable teenager and I came out a hardened brutal young man, a dangerous thug. And they didn't get me ready gently for my release by giving me town visits and home leave; they just spat me out once they'd chewed me up. Try to see through the anger in my words as I'm now past the stage of hating the system, I'm just telling it how it was and there is no other way of putting it.

What a wonderful day, the sun shining brightly, every prison officer waving a kid goodbye, all pats on the back and handshakes. What a fairy tale. I hated every screw, doctor and nurse except Mr Stevens. I've told you how harsh my life was in that prison unit, but I'd spent two years there and it was my home. I was scared stiff of the outside world. Yes, I wanted to be released but I was really frightened of leaving the unit as it was my comfort zone. I hadn't seen a car or bus in all that time, I hadn't even walked on grass, smelt nice smells, stroked a dog, crossed a road, paid for something in a shop. I didn't know how to do the smallest task after my breakdown, and I hadn't been around my family for three years. I was a stranger.

I was going back to live at my Mum's house and believe me it was going to be a long hard road from there on. Imagine my paranoia in the outside world, how would I be able to keep tabs on every enemy that crept into my mind on the out? At least most of the people I was paranoid about were stuck on the unit with me, but now on the street how would I know where my enemies were, they would be able to get to me whenever they wanted? I didn't have the security of a cell and a big steel door to protect me anymore.

Mr Stevens signed-in to work on the day of my release so he would be able to walk me to reception. That morning I woke at four o'clock and couldn't sleep any longer, so I read half a book to kill the time. The cell door opened at eight, it was time to go home. Mr Stevens had been my saviour for two years and was waiting for me, he could see in my eyes that I was scared, he was an experienced officer, he knew the deal, he knew how hard I'd find it on the out.

Within five minutes I was at reception, I changed into my own clothes which I hadn't worn for years; I remember them smelling dusty and old. I'd grown so much the Nike bottoms were like ankle swingers. With one last handshake I said goodbye to Mr Stevens, it was hard to take that I'd never see him again. But now it was time to look ahead, I walked out of the main gate and breathed in the fresh Buckinghamshire air. I was met by my brother-in-law and within minutes we were heading down the motorway to South London.

CHAPTER 7

Home Sweet Home

I felt sick as the car sped down the motorway. It was three years since I'd been in the fast lane. The trees looked greener, the buses brand spanking new. Dull prison landings impact your mind. Beyond the wall life is altogether more colourful. What's more, no longer the smell of piss, no more bleached floors. I stuck my head out of the window and sucked in a mouthful of air.

'I'm free you bastards! ... I've survived, fuck the system,' I screamed with pleasure. But it was foolish to believe freedom would be some sort of joyride. In one way Aylesbury would never leave me, it left wounds that will never totally heal. What lay ahead was anger, confusion, and pain. My next journey would be dark. There might be laughter but there would be tears. I was again heading into a pitch-black tunnel; maybe if I got my eyes tested I'd see the light. I'd rarely left my prison unit for over two years. Can you believe it I was expected to jump into line with everyday people?

I was to live at my mother's house which in my confused mind was my next prison. Because I'd been institutionalised my bedroom was a cell and my mother a prison officer. Fucked-up, wasn't I? Welcome to the mind of an unstable young man on prison licence. I entered my new cell, no bars on the windows, no pipe running through it to chat to pals at night. 'Shit the door's wooden, no lock, this is dangerous. The killers, the killers can get to me. Mission one, arm yourself for protection ... Guv, Guv, I mean Mum, Mum, can I come out to use the toilet?' 'You don't have to ask just go there, you live here, you're not in jail.'

Why was she being nice to me? Screws are never nice. People are not nice, every single person including my Mum is a threat to my life! I walked down the stairs and saw a middle-aged man sitting there; it was my neighbour George. I was suspicious. Was he a mate of Wayne Lister from the wing at Aylesbury coming to get me. I quickly went to the toilet and checked for escape routes, the bathroom window was too small. I'd gone from a seven stone streak of piss to eleven-and-a-half stone during three years in the slammer. As I walked back to my bedroom I took a knife from the kitchen drawer. I was laughing now, I'd cut any of them killers if they came for me.

My bedroom was my cell, my cell was my safety. I was too paranoid to go back downstairs to the toilet, so I started to piss out of the window, or in bottles. Yes, ridiculous but messed-up I was. My mother thought I was disgusting, but how was I to explain to her or anyone else how damaged I really was. Because in that state of mind this sort of behaviour was normal to me. It is only when I look back now that I can see how hard it was to adjust to normal life after being caged in a unit full of the country's worst young offenders who had done some of the most horrific crimes. Now I was meant to sit at the dinner table and eat a Sunday roast with my family. I just stared at the sprouts wondering who these other human beings were; I was like a wild animal they'd brought home. It wasn't long before I was kicking-off, and self-harming in my bedroom. My mother had expected her long lost son to come home a changed man, a son she could be proud of, but I was one messed-up freak.

I had to report to my probation officer once a week. You can get lucky and end-up with a decent one, but through my eyes I was unlucky, and I genuinely hated her. All that pain and humiliation those prison screws had put me through had me bursting at the seams with hatred towards any type of authority. Memories of being stripped naked and hosed down in the segregation block haunted me and I carried that darkness with me every day. Any person above me was deemed a prison officer, any threatening young man Wayne Lister.

My probation officer was really a prison officer out to destroy me and I hated her. When every other line of hers was recall to prison this, recall to prison that it didn't help my paranoia, so I believed she was evil, and that at any opportunity she wanted to send me back to jail to rot, where I belonged.

I was so angry back then towards the system. If I ever spotted a screw going about their business, I screamed abuse at them. 'You aren't in charge now, you aren't with your mob,' I'd shout. They would never say anything back of course; not without an army to back them up. To be filled with so much anger and hate is draining; it is a horrible place to be. The only way forward was to take a deep breath and try to let it all go, to move on. But at this stage there was plenty of mayhem to come before someone knocked sense into me.

I was told I needed to find a job, and that by law I'd to tell the employer I'd a criminal record and had just been released from prison. Searching through the local paper I found an advert for a 'grass cutter.' 'Wow,' I thought, 'you actually get paid for cutting grasses' but this wasn't a snitches-get-stitches service. I was to find it was more of a gardening job, not sorting out telltales.

I was still on heavy anti-psychotic medication; olanzapene was its name, making you fat and slow. I sat drugged-up and like a zombie in front of this Bill Oddie-looking bloke and told him I was a strong, fit young man and I'd really love to trim hedges and blow leaves down the road. As he took notes, I looked around the portacabin and noticed lawn mowers, garden shears and other sharp objects. But back to the interrogation, I mean interview. 'Any other things I should know about you, Justin?' In slurred speech I told him I'd just been released from prison. 'Oh, ok, shouldn't be too much of an issue, what was it for?' 'Well you see, I sort of attacked two men on the Underground with a meat cleaver and served three years out of four-and-a half for it.' Just picture the look on Bill's face in an awkward moment. For some strange reason I didn't get the job, not even a call back or reason why.

My next employment attempt was to become a dustman, I've never under-stood why I didn't get that job either, I'm sure I was capable of slinging rubbish into a dustcart. To get rejected for that job was like being punched in the guts, that really dented my confidence. With no job and no money, I was a proper waster, rotting away in my bedroom. 'Fuck the medication.' I stopped taking those mind control pills and started sipping Grandpas 'cough medicine' instead. Drunk as a skunk I was and even more reckless.

Mum had a new boyfriend and to me he was an intruder, he wasn't good for her. I knew he feared me. Can you blame him, I was a nasty, damaged young man? The final straw came when in my messed-up state of mind I threatened to kill him … and Mum. Yes, disgusting and now it was time for me to be kicked-out of her house. In my crazy state of mind I believed they were prison officers, the punishment block-type. Just like I'd have done back in Aylesbury I threatened to stab them. Mum was so scared she moved all the sharp knives out of the house. She couldn't understand what was going through my head, no-one could and that's sad. I was suffering, but in the eyes of everyone else I was a nutcase.

I had nowhere to go but I'd always been a street kid, so the streets were now to become my home once again. I'd slept in some real grim places as a teen, burnt out cars, bushes, under railway bridges and in squats. One of my favourite places was the local bus depot. When I was a boy the night staff would let me sleep on the unused buses deep at the back. So, with my brain frozen in time for three years during my incarceration I immediately headed there. Buses were five-star hotels compared to some places.

I don't understand how as a small boy I never felt the cold, but now as a 21-year-old I found sleeping rough unbearable. I was cold, broke and lonely. 'Is curling-up on a bus seat what I waited three fucking years for?' I asked myself, 'I should have given it up a long time ago.' Each morning I scraped together 40p for a cup of tea in the local café to warm myself up for the start of another day wandering the pavements. I'm sure people I bumped into from my younger days looked on in disgust; I was too weak to care or even stare back at them. If I was hungry, I'd steal sandwiches from the local bakers or fruit from the supermarket.

For a while a friend called Verb joined me in the bus garage, it was like having a cellmate. One day whilst walking for what seemed like miles, we came across a hedgehog. Fascinated with our spiky friend we let him roll-up in a cardboard box and took him with us. Now there were three of us banged-up on our bus and in the morning the two of us made a quick exit before it went into service. I've often pictured the look on the passengers faces as they sat for their usually boring journey finding a hedgehog 'fare dodging.'

When I left Aylesbury Prison my psychologist, Rachel, wrote a report recommending I receive ongoing mental health support. Did I receive it? I was living in a garage so there's your answer! Looking back now, for me to be living on the streets was disgusting. But what could I do, what could probation do? After many battles with my probation officer, she managed to get me to agree to be placed in a hostel for the night on the basis that I return to my local council in the morning to sign the relevant papers to get me a permanent place. Though I was only there for one night I hated it, most of the residents were on drugs or up to skullduggery. I woke in my usual negative frame of mind and instead of going straight to the council I wandered out and stole a large bottle of vodka. Now pissed and late for my appointment I strolled past a market stall selling BB pellet guns. The overweight trader was too busy trying to chat up a young blonde when in no time I swiped one of them and was off. Though it only fired pellets it was an exact copy of a Beretta M9 pistol. With it in my waist band I carried on with my day.

What the hell was I going to do with a gun in the state of mind I was in. I think you may have guessed I wasn't about to go and shoot cola cans off a wall. 'If only it was real,' I thought, 'I could shoot some of the bastards who've hurt me, put me down and abused me.' Thinking better of it I left the BB gun at a friend's house and forgot about it for a while.

Probation were seriously upset with me for not signing the paperwork, but I didn't give a fuck. 'I'll go back and live with my friend Verb anyway,' I thought in my crazed state. I got back to the room to find the hostel boss had broken down the door and removed my goods. I was not welcome. It was cold outside and I was so tired. We barricaded ourselves in the room using the bed and a cupboard hoping we could get a roof over our heads for one more night. It must have been around two in the morning when the hostel boss and two police officers started booting down the door. That was it, half asleep we headed back to the bus garage.

My days were now spent shoplifting for food money and the evenings looking for shelter. I went to prison a lost boy and now I was a lost young man. I used to lie on that cell mattress for years dreaming of better things and they amounted to this. I was judged harshly and as 'trouble' by family and friends but I needed some love and support in my life. Nobody could see that I was not only institutionalised but mentally unwell. In some narrow minded people's eyes I was just a bad lot. Like the eyes of those who looked down their noses at hoodies on the street corner. 'No-one is born bad, something turned them that way,' I convinced myself.

I started to hang around with local street kids; they were between the ages of 15 and 17. And here I was a grown man knocking around with them. From the outside it might have looked strange, but my mindset was that of a 17-year-old street kid. Before jail all I knew was to be in a gang on my local streets. I tried to find peace and an answer to my inner fears that way now. But deep down it was just embarrassing. Vodka killed that feeling for a while. This happens to many young offenders who go in-and-out of prison, their mind becomes frozen in time, and they get older and older still hanging around on the streets. And these kids were nothing like my teenage gang. This new generation were cuddly puppies compared to my crew. Back then we were like a pack of bloodthirsty wolves.

One good thing about knocking around with this crowd however was that my cousin Chanelle was the main girl in the group. It felt good to be around a friendly family member after all of these years. But it was to end badly. She was drinking a lot and going off the rails and though I didn't encourage this I was to blame in the eyes of older family members. This hurt like hell, I'd never influence my younger cousin and, if anything, I was around to protect her. I knew the streets better than any of this mob, so I was her eyes and ears.

Whilst sitting in a pub my phone rang. 'Help, help Justin, help me.' It was Chanelle. A fight had broken out with some local girls and in the heat of the moment somebody had passed her a knife and she'd stabbed a rival in the stomach, seriously injuring her. Confused and scared about what she'd done, Chanelle had dialed my number crying for help. A group of local youths were chasing her to avenge her attack on their friend. She was lucky I was around and just a short sprint away. I got there faster than Usain Bolt on Red Bull to be confronted by an angry mob baying for her blood. Immediately my old survival tactics and hypervigilance kicked in. Empty a bin, find a bottle, smash it for the intimidating sound it makes, then look the enemy straight in the eye, to let them know I'd cut any of them who got closer. I'd used this tactic many times over the years. It didn't matter if I was outnumbered, swinging a sharp object and showing no fear meant I was likely to win against the odds. With that they were gone. I believe I saved my cousin from a beating that night and who knows what might have happened, maybe she could have been killed if I hadn't showed up. What Chanelle did was wrong, but blood is thicker than water and I had to protect her.

Afterwards Chanelle couldn't handle what she'd done and tried to take her own life. I went to see her in hospital. It was a sad sight to see her in a state. When she got better she moved away. I was 'obviously to blame' for her behaviour and the entire family were judging me once again. Other relatives were told, 'Don't tell Justin where Chanelle is' and so on. I felt like a monster. I also felt cheated that she never contacted me for years after the drama we'd been through together. I thought we were close and to be treated like that only added to my destructive nature. 'No-one gives a fuck about me, no-one cares' was my view of life.

Why was history repeating itself, why wasn't I part of normal society? I'd always felt like the black sheep, the outcast. I was hurting inside with no-one to hold, no shoulder to cry on. The pain from being in prison was eating away at me, the flashbacks of Aylesbury killing me. Didn't any of these people understand the horrors I'd been through in there? 'Hell mate, like hell I tell you, I've seen a small corner of hell.' Now I was about to be arrested for breach of my licence and I can tell you I wasn't about to just stroll back to that corner. No with a capital N, I'd avoid prison at all costs. I wasn't exactly Harrison Ford in 'The Fugitive' but none the less I was on the run ...

CHAPTER 8

Meet Jimmy Walker the Stalker

A round this time, I met a girl called Sarah. They say opposites attract and we were definitely opposites. We came from different ends of Carshalton, me from the St Helier Estate, once the largest in Southern England. If you picture Surrey as all leafy, green and smart you'd be wrong, my end wasn't a pretty picture. Sarah came from Carshalton Beeches the posh part. I don't like to use the word class as I believe humanity shouldn't be put into categories, we all breathe the same air, we're all the same in my eyes. But when I was growing-up, Carshalton was a word spoken in hushed tones unless you added Beeches.

Sarah went to private school. I never went to school at all if I could help it. She had a warm home, I was a street kid, she went to work, I went out pinching and so on. One day I went on a shoplifting spree and decided to take some designer glasses, in fact five pairs. God knows why. Afterwards we headed to a friend's house, only for him to appear with the BB gun I'd left there (that I mentioned in the last chapter). I'd totally forgotten about it. It was damaged and the pellets were gone. I quickly claimed it back and tucked it into my waistband. We left the house and by extremely bad timing an unmarked police car came screeching to a halt. Butterflies hit my stomach and adrenalin took over. 'A right sticky moment,' I thought to myself, adding a four-letter word, 'What with a gun in my belt, a knife in my pocket and five pairs of stolen glasses. God, I'm nicked and back to jail, back to that hell-hole!'

Without a second thought I ran for it, my heart pumping as I sprinted away. As I hit the street corner I reached for the gun and threw it over a fence into a building site. I carried on running, getting out of breath and slower and slower. I looked back and I saw an officer jump into a builder's van for a lift. I bet that builder felt like a right hero and I hated that kind of hero! I threw the knife in a bush and in the process cut my hand. All of a sudden 'bang' the builder and the copper leapt on top of me. I was nicked. My initial thoughts were, 'I hope they don't find the weapons,' but to my disappointment a helpful bystander had seen me throw the gun and the police found it. I was arrested for possession of a firearm and theft. They never found the knife which would have meant an extra charge to add to the already growing list.

Back at the police station I was shown the gun which had been opened-up and inspected by the Metropolitan Police Trojan Unit and at first glance I didn't even think it was mine, but it really did look real. Trojan had checked to see if it had been converted to fire real bullets, which would have carried a minimum of five years in prison. Back then, I wondered what all the fuss was about. 'It fires pellets for fuck's sake. Usually plastic ones,' I thought. But due to the rising number of converted firearms on London's streets they had to check. I lay in my cell and prayed for bail. That cell had probably heard thousands of prayers by men that were non-religious in their everyday life. It's funny how we commit sins daily but in our most self-inflicted, desperate hours we start praying to a man we don't believe in. 'Maybe God is real,' I told myself as I was informed that I was to be released on bail. I was charged with possessing an imitation firearm and handling stolen goods. I grinned once again at my luck. I had strict bail conditions: to live at my mother's house under curfew and to report to the police twice a week. 'Oh boy,' I thought as I smiled inside. Most nights were now spent staying in with Sarah, which was good for me. But I didn't know how to have a relationship. With no money and her birthday coming up I figured I'd need to steal money to buy her some trainers that she wanted.

Whilst chilling-out in front of the TV my phone started ringing. It was from an unknown caller. A male voice screamed down the phone that he'd been sleeping with Sarah, my girlfriend, and that she loved him not me. Obviously disturbed by the call I confronted her. She denied it fully and told me Jim her ex-boyfriend wouldn't stop pestering her. As you can imagine my paranoia went through the roof, not because of Sarah, I believed her, but I now had a new enemy.

Prison flashbacks came flooding into my head and I was convinced her ex wouldn't give-up pestering her, and I was correct. One night we noticed a young man hanging around outside my mother's home and, when Sarah looked, she told me that it was a friend of Jim's. 'This is a fucking liberty,' I thought, 'him coming to my mother's place' so in true prisoner fashion I grabbed a knife, went outside and started chasing him, but he escaped. Looking back, I'm glad he did. I was so dangerous I'd probably have caused him real harm.

I was angry at Sarah for bringing trouble into my life, but I started to realise she was petrified of Jimmy Walker and his gang. She was a quiet, easily lead girl who lived a sheltered life and was not used to violence or threats like I'd encountered many times in my young life. Jimmy Walker was Irish with a thick mop of ginger hair, and he hated the fact that she'd left him or me.

Jimmy Walker is my rhyming slang for 'stalker' as I don't want you to know his real name. Sarah started to get unwanted calls day and night. I watched as she became more and more anxious. My thoughts were always of seeing to this parasite, 'How dare he terrorise her.' Up to ten pizza deliveries a day would turn up at her home, cabs would arrive frequently. Jimmy lived way away in Essex but nonetheless he started to turn up at her workplace and hung around there looking intimidating. Every time she changed her number he'd find the new one, and I figured this was down to it being passed on by so-called friends. The stalking stepped up a gear when a brick flew through her bedroom window.

One morning my sister went outside to find her car had been attacked by vandals with paint stripper. It's deadly if poured on a car, absolutely ruins the paintwork. I've always had a dislike for people who damage another's home or car out of spite or a grudge; it's a cowardly way to hurt their victim. I knew straightaway it was Jimmy Walker but how on earth did he find out where my sister lived? Within the next couple of weeks all of her family's cars were damaged with paint stripper. My paranoia went through the roof; I tried to stay away from her thinking this would get rid of it. But how could I just leave Sarah all alone to deal with this demon. Jimmy quickly became the new Wayne Lister, but unlike Lister he was free to roam the streets. No brick walls and steel doors between us for protection.

Sarah's family contacted the police many times, but like a lot of stalking cases not a lot got done back then. The phone calls kept coming and coming. Due to some experiences with the occult and Devil worship as a vulnerable teen I was convinced the Devil was out to get me. In my head it was easy to see Jimmy as a man controlled by demons and evil. Whilst walking through my local high street I was approached by a young man talking of God and how with Jesus on my side I'd be cleansed of my sins. I'd find peace. I'll tell you now, this book is not about to turn into a bible bashing session, but in my distorted frame of mind I wondered what it would be like to praise the lord.

That Sunday I attended a gospel church and listened to speeches from an American pastor on how Jesus saves those who repent. 'Does anybody want Him to save them today?' he asked in a deafening American deep South accent. Anxiously I found my hand waving in the air, like I wasn't in control of my limbs. The guy I'd met in the high street was whispering something to the pastor and next thing I knew I found myself out in front of the congregation on my knees. The pastor put his hand on my head and screamed, 'Lord release these demons from this boy, Devil we rebuke you ... Devil release yourself.'

The whole church was told to pray for me. I rose to my feet and was asked whether I felt any different, I think I was meant to feel at peace, but all I felt was anxiety. 'You can't heal PTSD just like that, no way!' I thought but I pretended that I felt amazing, and was now saved. I screamed 'Hallelujah!' and they all started clapping. 'What the fuck,' I thought,' these folk are madder than me.'

I would have liked to have walked from that church a new man, but I looked in the mirror and saw the same old Justin. I tried my best to be a born-again Christian for around 48 hours, I'd lived my whole life sinning and now was expected to be cleansed. My paranoia worsened, 'Shit I can't have sex before marriage, that's not right ... I'm going to hell for sinning.' Then it was, 'Shit, I can't listen to rap music,' so I switched on Magic FM and was confronted by Sting's 'Fields of Gold.' I thought, 'Fuck me, I'm going mental.' In no time I'd my headphones in and had converted back to Devil music and the evil that goes with it. I was again walking in hellfire.

That night I chilled with Sarah and with our phones turned-off we had an evening of peace, away from Jimmy Walker's disturbing calls. We relaxed with candles and watched some skinhead rant and rave on the box. As the candlelight flickered, I noticed the light shining on my rap albums and I was reminded of my sinning. After a while we decided to head to the supermarket to grab some food and drinks. I remember passing a friend's house, trying to decide whether to visit him or not. Fate was on my side when I thought, 'Ah, better not.'

As I entered the house, I could smell smoke. I rushed upstairs to find flames hitting the ceiling of my room. Panic took over and I started to fill a bucket with water. I then realised that I'd left a candle burning, which had caused a speaker and my rap albums to catch fire. It was too late, the water did nothing, and me and Sarah ran from the house dialing 999. I was extremely anxious once again. In my confused mental state I believed that this was some sort of act of God, as punishment for turning back to the Devil. Looking back, I obviously don't believe that to be correct, I was just attracting so much negativity into my life as I was such a negative young man. But when I spoke of my theory to churchgoers, they believed that yes I'd been burnt for my sins. This didn't help my troubles. I remember Mum's nosey neighbours looking on in disbelief as smoke poured down the usually quiet street. The firemen managed to put out the flames, but my room was a pile of ash. Anything that was not hit by the flames was either smoke-damaged or waterlogged.

The fire was so hot it melted the double glazing. Every wall and ceiling in the house was black from smoke. I was gutted. My mother was away, and I was only staying there on bail. But now because of my devilish ways God had burnt her house down. Mental isn't it, well welcome to my life, a bit like 'Eastenders' on crystal meth, only I'm more handsome than Phil Mitchell.

I didn't have a penny to fix things. I had to go out on a thieving spree to at least try to replace a few things before my Mum got back from holiday. One thing I wish I'd never done was throw my prison poetry away. I'd written around 600 poems during my three years or so of being banged-up, and whilst searching for anything to salvage from the ashes I found the box they were kept in. Though waterlogged I'm sure I could have dried them out, but I threw them away, lying to myself, saying they were wrecked. In reality my OCD wanted them out, as they came from Aylesbury Prison and I couldn't touch a thing from that hell-hole; in my eyes they had Wayne Lister's energy all over them.

I found out that Sarah was pregnant yet I couldn't just be over the moon. How the hell could I look after a child when I couldn't even look after myself. And with a trial coming up at court I didn't even know if I'd be around to become a father. I was going to plead not guilty to possession of an imitation firearm due to the fact that these weapons are legal to buy throughout the UK and you're allowed to transport them from place to place, or so I thought. I'd heard stories of armed police throwing kids on the floor for firing BB guns, only to have them confiscated and sent on their way without being arrested. So why the hell was I going to be found guilty when there was no evidence to say

I wasn't taking it from my friend's back to my home legally. But why would I run off if I'd nothing to hide? Because I had stolen goods on my person!

I thought I stood a good chance of getting a not guilty verdict and, with the case staying in Wimbledon Magistrates' Court, if I was found guilty the sentence would be low. So here we were once again, I was back up in court to fight for my future. I and my witnesses did well, but not that well as I was found guilty. The magistrate pointed out that this was due to me running away, acting in a suspicious manner. So now it ends hey? Back to prison? Stuff that, I'd other plans.

Without a second thought I jumped over the dock knocking the holy books flying and shoving the court clerk aside as I headed out of the courtroom. To my surprise there was no security around. I casually walked-off not wishing to raise suspicion … and then ran for my life. I didn't look back; I just jumped a high wall down into Wimbledon Railway Station, leapt on a train and got the fuck out of there. I'd escaped my immediate fate, no I wasn't going back to jail for anyone. I was free! Or was I? Being on the run wasn't freedom. The initial buzz faded faster than a British summer.

CHAPTER 9

Running

It's not good being a wanted man. 'Now where do I go?' I wondered. The first night I stayed at Sarah's parent's home. 'What a wicked hideout,' I told myself, and yes it was. She being pregnant her family took me in. They knew nothing of my criminal past or that I was on the run and I felt at peace staying there knowing I wasn't linked to that address. I think they felt I'd protect Sarah and them from her stalker. In the meantime, the cops were keeping tabs on my mother's house, and most nights knocking at relatives addresses in pursuit of this madman you've come to know.

Sutton police soon found out about my whereabouts and informed Sarah's parent's of my colourful past and that I'd escaped from court. I was not around when the boys in blue showed-up, and I never returned there to face capture. After her family found out about my background I'm sure they wanted their daughter to disown me. She could do a lot better in their eyes I guess. But how could she when she was having my child? Let's just say her father lent me some money to find my feet and with that I rented the grimiest flat that was so cold the cockroaches wore body warmers and so damp the mice went around in speedboats. But it was a roof over my head.

The police were back and forth searching for me and also for Jimmy Walker who, having replaced Wayne Lister inside my crazy head, was still turning up to harass Sarah on a regular basis. I lay in my new home dreaming of my girlfriend and of having a child, but you see things were never that simple for me. As soon as I started to feel comfortable for this once, it was cruelly snatched away and I was on my own again. I moved to a completely different location, deeper in South London, a place popular with people from diverse backgrounds,

Indian, Sri-Lankan, African, Jamaican and so on. You could say it was slightly different from my usual stomping ground, which was predominately white. It doesn't take a genius to work out why I switched boroughs. Around my old turf I stood out like a sore thumb; five feet eleven inches tall, of mixed race, covered in scars and tattoos, I couldn't just blend in. Though the new manor was as rough as hell, I could disappear, and it was great to once again try the kind of food I'd shared with Nathan and the Tamils.

Life was a lot faster in this London borough, and you didn't say 'Hi' to the neighbours when you went to collect your morning paper and pint of milk. Downstairs was a crack addict. Late at night I'd hear strange goings on, screams, mumbling noises, banging, sometimes fights, occasionally what sounded like group sex, all sorts. My flat wasn't exactly Fort Knox; I didn't feel secure, so I slept with a weapon next to me. If those maniacs kicked in my door I had to be ready.

The money Sarah's father gave me to get on my feet wasn't going to last long, but at this point I was sure he would continue helping me out if I needed it. I couldn't work: I still suffered from anxiety and found it hard to socialise with normal people; and I couldn't use my National Insurance number as the police would track me down. The same reason I couldn't sign-on and claim benefits. I knew several people who'd been on the run and made the mistake of signing-on out of desperation and were then bundled off to jail by five burly coppers, all for a measly 40 quid a week!

So, my days were wasted lying on a crusty old mattress watching TV, a bit like being in prison again only this time with mice for company, not the sociable type either, they stared at me for a split second then legged it. Some evenings Sarah would come over to visit me and, if I was lucky, she'd bring a bag of food from the shops, with treats such as crisps, fizzy drinks and sweets. I know she never felt safe in that environment, coming from a lovely home, and now she was visiting a mice infested flat in a ghetto.

On a few occasions I headed back into the wanted zone when I was like one of the SAS; well at least I thought I was. I'd sit at a crowded bus stop so I could hide my face. I'd wait patiently as commuters made their way off the bus and quickly run in by the back door without paying. Most of the time the driver never saw me, otherwise it was back to the bus stop to wait for the next one. I'd always be on the lookout for undercover police, hard to spot, but not impossible. I called them 'undies' for short, or Ted Bundys, rhyming slang and after the American serial killer.

One day, my friend Gordon and I decided to bunk a train to Surrey. As a commuter entered the barrier, we slid through for free and I noticed our man of the moment Jimmy Walker in the crowd. I guessed he was heading for Sarah's place, Essex where he lived being miles away. 'He can only be going to stalk her,' I told myself. Anger boiled deep within me as I blocked his path, the first time I'd come face-to-face with this parasite who'd tried to ruin my life and stolen my girlfriend's confidence, leaving us all with anxiety.

'You're Jimmy Walker ... aren't you?' I asked aggressively and he replied, 'Get the fuck out of my way.' With that I punched him hard in the face. I'm not Mohammed Ali but he dropped to the floor in a heap. A woman commuter ran to us shouting at me to stop. I'd seen red and as I snapped out of it I could hear her screams as she tried to protect him saying, 'Leave him alone, you coward.' Through my blurred vision I noticed Jimmy's two phones lying on the platform. Without thinking I picked them up, ran out of the station and jumped onto a nearby bus.

The police never knew the background to all this only what they saw from the CCTV, Justin Rollins a wanted and violent criminal beating an innocent young man — and yes, he saw the opportunity to stitch me up by telling them he never knew his attacker and had been robbed because he was an easy target. As I started to search his phones I found my own number stored as 'Dead' next to which Sarah's was under 'Slag.' The caller list went on, he had my mother's landline number, Sarah's parents' phone, Gordon's, my sister's and even my church friends' numbers. 'Very strange,' I thought.

Next, I looked at his text messages, hundreds on each phone. I felt sickened as I saw them, most were death threats he'd sent to Sarah, many of a disturbed sexual nature. He had inbox messages from an unknown number explaining to him where best to buy paint stripper. Can you believe it, I was sitting there with the evidence needed to convict this pest. 'What can I do' I asked myself 'hand them to the police and be arrested?' I couldn't give the details to Sarah's parents even though they were in regular contact with the police about Jimmy. How could they say, 'Right we now have proof of what Jimmy's been doing, only problem is our daughter's new boyfriend beat the shit out of him to get it?' He was laughing whilst we all still suffered.

Upon further inspection I found photos of a couple that looked a bit too familiar. My heart skipped a beat as I realised they were of Sarah and me in a restaurant. The thought of him watching us sent a shiver down my spine. I could deal with the odd psychopath in prison but this was a whole new level. Stalkers are often cunning, all about control, their lives revolve around their victims, and they eat, sleep and breathe harassment. Some take it to the ultimate level, killing. You only have to look at the news. Sarah's case was nothing compared to the story of one crazed stalker who walked into his former workplace at Harvey Nichols store in West London and shot his victim several times in the head before turning the gun on himself. He'd already admitted a charge of harassment towards her and was due to be sentenced for that offence only days later. Thankfully these cases are rare. But none the less 'ordinary' cases still leave the victim and family in fear and misery.

After the attack I made it safely back to my hideout and lay on my mattress with a hundred and one thoughts buzzing around inside my head. 'Shit, I'm gonna be nicked … Shit he's going to seek revenge on Sarah.' What a bloody mess I was in. I needed to speak to her fast. I explained how I'd beaten Jimmy, but I knew it was far from over. She told me the police had been to her house looking for me yet again and that they now knew about the connection between Jimmy and me. But it was too late; I couldn't hand over the evidence of him stalking her, as out of anger I'd thrown the phones away. 'What's the point?' I thought, 'that bastard's won. I'm the one on CCTV committing an attack on him?' I started smashing-up my flat in sheer desperation and to be honest after I'd finished the place still looked the same bloody dump!

Sarah sobbing through a flood of tears told me she couldn't handle the double stress of being stalked and her future baby's father on the run. With that she hung up. 'Doesn't anyone know of my pain?' I screamed out loud. I then heard banging from downstairs, from the crack house and with that I started banging back, screaming abuse at the floorboards. 'You bastards, you're all bastards,' I shouted as I punched the floor with my bare knuckles causing them to bleed and get splinters. But at that point I only felt the mental pain, the physical pain didn't matter. Nothing mattered; 'Everyone's against me,' I told to myself.

Next day I woke up in a state and didn't care what day it was or what time. I phoned Sarah and all I heard was screaming and crying. 'It's over, it's over,' she said. 'Don't say that,' I told her, 'I've no-one now, what about our baby?' We were both crying, we both felt extreme pain, maybe for different reasons. Her from being stalked and me because I was about to lose the one bit of happiness I'd experienced in many years after my time in a concrete jungle.

She told me the devastating news she'd had a miscarriage due to the stress and worry. In her own words she'd sat on the toilet 'dripping blood.' My child was now no more than blood down a fucking toilet. Pain, more fucking pain. That's all I felt: the thought of Sarah crying on the toilet, the thought of Jimmy laughing, of me going back to prison. Other thoughts raced through my mind, if I'd had a gun then I'd have just blown my brains across the room. 'I know, I should just jump in front of a train. The driver probably wouldn't even stop.' I was at one of the lowest points of my life and as you know I've quite a few to choose from.

Sarah told me she was heading to the hospital and would speak to me later. So, I sat alone and thought of how Jimmy had killed my child, well in that state of mind I couldn't come to any 'normal' conclusions. 'Fuck the stress; it's never-ending in my life,' I thought. I waited and waited for Sarah's call, but it never came. Worried about her I went to the phone box with the few coins I had left. The first attempt went to voicemail, the second I got an answer. It was her father. 'Can I speak to Sarah please?' I asked politely. 'Look Sarah doesn't want to talk to you at the moment, we are just not used to this type of life, it's over.' With that he hung up.

'Just not used to this,' I thought to myself. Like I was fucking used to being on the run, praying for better days, dreaming of having a beautiful child only to be told it had been lost. My heart had been ripped from my chest. I felt cheated; at that point I hated Sarah, her parents and everybody else for ruining my hopeless life.

I never tried to phone Sarah after that, in fact I didn't speak to anyone for days. I must have lost around a stone due to not eating and stress. I couldn't look at myself in the mirror; I stared around that shit hole of a flat and wondered if I'd be better off in jail, or even worse dead. I finally turned on my phone after three days to find a text from Sarah saying she wanted to meet me, so we arranged to do this. It felt strange looking at her after all that had happened; there weren't any hugs or any emotional stuff. She'd only come to hand me £200 from her father to help me out and then she was gone again. I was grateful for the money but in truth I felt cheated or even cheap to be honest.

Like her family had paid me off. You know given me a little bit of money hoping everything would be okay. Hoping I'd become a distant memory and they could get on with their cozy life in their nice home in Carshalton Beeches.

I was a bitter young man and obviously I had reasons to be. Sarah and her family were going through shit too. They lived in fear of Jimmy and the stress from the police looking for me. They didn't know how to deal with it. I guess we just coped in different ways. Sarah's dad was a good man; he worked hard, loved his family and would try to help anyone. He was what I'd call a proper gentleman, and I was definitely not at all gentle or proper. If I'd been him, I wouldn't have wanted someone like me around my daughter!

Two hundred pounds doesn't last too long in the real world, and after my next rent payment I was broke again. No food in the fridge and as a matter of fact I didn't even have a plate to eat from. I remember having pasta out of the pan using a wooden spoon. With no-one to help me out it was back to the streets doing what I knew best, crime.

Unable to claim benefits in my own name and get my rent paid, I convinced my friend, Gordon, to move in with me and do this. I convinced G (as I call him) that he was getting older and needed freedom from his parents and he agreed. G was a messed-up guy like me, who spent time in my gang as a teenager and through my years in prison he didn't move on in life. He sat at home smoking weed and getting high to the point that he wanted some excitement. That is what I was offering him, so that when he saw the cold, dirty flat that I was living in he didn't really care. He saw it as our bachelor pad in his crazed mind. Another bonus of being with G was that he drove me around, together we were double trouble. We would travel at high speed through the South London traffic weaving in and out of bus lanes and red routes, knowing full well no-one would know his address or that he didn't have a licence or insurance. We were reckless but didn't give a damn. If I saw us today, I'd look the other way, we oozed trouble!

Sarah and Jimmy were far from my mind as I channelled my anger and pain into becoming a thug and troublemaker. My hatred for the prison system ran deep and I soon got the initials FTS for 'Fuck The System' tattooed on my neck. My body was becoming covered in tattoos. I had 36 on my neck as 'three six' was like the mark of the beast and I had 'Angel of Death' there as well. My arms had reminders of prison, over some of the scars I'd the words 'Until death do us part' and a Grim Reaper on my chest. With a shiny shaved head and scars across my face I cut a menacing character. I'd started shaving my head aged just 16 after becoming a fan of a crazy rapper called Sticky Fingaz. He rapped on guns and drugs but also other stuff like trying to electrocute himself. His character fitted my wild side and I wanted to be him back in my teens. Now with a shaved head, scars from over the years, the tattoos and multiple gold teeth (to imitate Southern rappers in the US) I was where I wanted to be. No Sarah, no baby, no responsibility!

I was a messed-up young man and, even though I used to be a street gang leader, I was now trying to be some sort of gangster. In reality, I was just lost, like many others I knew I was trying to live up to an image. Wiser people knew real gangsters didn't drive around without driving licenses and they weren't involved in petty crime. The real wise guys were sitting on millions while their henchmen did the dirty work. They weren't standing on the street corner or trying to show off to their fake friends. No, the real gangster was a business-man, the suited and booted character in the background. The one that nobody hears about, living the good life, sipping cocktails on a beach in the Caribbean.

While we were driving through our local streets our music was always on full volume. Music had such an impact on my mind, like I'm sure it has on many other people, but as you are aware I wasn't the sort of person who was into rock 'n roll. I didn't spend my teenage years at festivals, concerts and gigs hav-ing fun with my friends. We would listen to homegrown Gangsta rap. Around this time London-bred musicians started to get noticed and teenage gangs and rappers posted their output on platforms like Channel U and YouTube. For the first time ever, London rappers would get their music out to a wider audience.

G and I listened to hardcore lyrics of violence, prison and crime. Notorious South London gangs dressed in hoodies and masks as they rapped. If it wasn't for the English accents you'd easily have mistaken them for hardcore LA Blood and Crip gang members. The reality was that these were young men just like us that lived only a short drive away. Due to this sort of rap finding an audience, the rappers, many who were from feared gangs, started to make DVDs. The crazy thing was that these were not just for promoting their music or rapping skills but to show off their guns. Dressed in bandanas and masks they waved their shotguns and handguns at the cameras. The DVDs would go on sale in underground music stores across the city. But it wasn't long before the Met's

Operation Trident set up to deal with black-on-black gun crime started fighting back by raiding these shops and shutting them down.

Watching these DVDs was shocking but appealing when feeling so alienated from society and angry at the system. Glamorising crime impressed us and influenced us yet more. One side of this stood out, the big aggressive dogs that the rappers had growling at the cameras. These images made immature minds feel good and we thought it was clever and that it would be a good way to raise our status and create fear. One day while G was on the street he bumped into two men walking pit bull-type dogs. He enquired where he could purchase one and the owner gave him a phone number and told him, 'Say you're a friend of Scotty.' It was time to get my own dog and of course I wasn't looking for man's best friend, rather a dangerous canine accessory to enhance my bad boy image. I'd also heard that there was money to be made from buying a bitch; a pit bull puppy could be sold for £200–£500.

I dialed the number, half expecting a Scottish voice to answer, but a street talking man picked-up, and he spoke my language. I immediately introduced myself as a friend of Scotty and was told to drive to a notorious council block in Peckham to collect a dog for £300. In Peckham I again dialed the number and was told to come further into the estate. Me and G waited patiently. After ten minutes a hooded man with a rucksack and a big-muscled pit bull appeared. The dog was on a long lead and, as the man came towards us, he made a whistling sound causing the dog to jump through the air towards us. He whistled again and the dog landed by our feet, sniffed around and didn't pay us much attention.

This was a test and we'd passed. If we'd jumped back in fear we could have been attacked. Because we didn't flinch at all we earned the respect of both man and dog. We shook hands and he pulled a tiny, sand-coloured pit bull bitch from the bag. After handing over the £300 the dog was ours and we named her Bella. After we'd paid, we relaxed, and he showed us the tricks that his own dog could pull off. I was amazed at how it could run up trees and flip off walls. I knew this man was the real deal and his dog would kill if he commanded. Even though I was attacked by a Doberman when I was a kid I never feared dogs and found aggressive dogs fascinating. The man told us about illegal dog fighting in Ireland and Birmingham and said to never let other people touch Bella as this would keep the dog loyal only to us. He said not to wash the dog, as having your dog smelling of roses would affect its own status amongst other dogs. Though hardened thugs we stood and believed everything he said.

As the weeks passed we made more trips to the man buying more pups which we then sold on for up to £600 each. It was easy money. Some of these pit bulls became family pets but on them escaping and the police rounding them up they were identified as a banned breed and destroyed. Others became aggressive and killed other dogs so were also put down.

We looked on Bella as a money-making machine. When ready to breed and if she produced say five puppies that was £2,500. Nowadays, I'm quite ashamed of that, because I love dogs. Back street breeding is a nasty way of making money, especially when the dogs end up in the hands of people like us! But at the time we didn't care. In our eyes Bella would make us rich, and to pay the rent we needed money. We always had one ear to the street about how to do this and were all the time exchanging numbers with other untrustworthy people.

G told me he had a 'move.' A move was a robbery or a way to make money and I was all ears. He had information that there was a cannabis factory harvesting hundreds of plants run by Vietnamese growers. The only thing was it was back over in Sutton borough and the police were looking for me, so even with the promise of making thousands my gut instinct said not to go there. G went off that evening and I stayed in the dirty flat with Bella. Come midnight he wasn't back so I decided to get some sleep. When I woke in the morning I checked his room and he wasn't there. I called his phone but every time it went to voicemail. Deep down I knew something had happened. I walked around the streets but couldn't find his car and after a couple of days decided to ask his mum if she'd heard from him. I made my way back to our flat full of worry. I was sure G wasn't dead, but I was also sure he must have been arrested or was being held somewhere.

CHAPTER 10

Bootlegging Days

Pirated DVDs were all too familiar on the streets of London. From afar this might look like a victimless crime. 'Where's the harm in buying a couple of films for a few measly quid?' you might ask. And if they happened to be good copies no doubt when the fella approached you again—with the latest Spiderman or James Bond, or maybe a blue movie (don't worry I won't tell the missus) — you might buy more. The fact is piracy has many victims and paying-out some of your hard-earned wages on a dodgy DVD helps fund organized crime.

During my time on the streets the bosses of this naughty little game were leaders of gangs such as Chinese Triads or Snakeheads, Japanese Yakuza or Italian Mafia gangs, who were almost untouchable due to their codes of silence. If you're picturing a few blokes with a DVD copier in their shed you're completely wrong. They were highly organized, bringing illegal immigrants into the country and forcing them to sell mass-produced fakes. Back then you'd find sellers approaching offices, pubs and even knocking at your front door. The sellers were held against their will in overcrowded houses and forced to pay for their unlawful passage. Refusal might lead to a beating and threats to harm their family back home. It's estimated that at its height this criminal activity was netting 500 million pounds a year in the UK alone, the profits 're-invested' in money laundering, unlicensed gambling, prostitution and other questionable activities.

The other victims were the companies who made the genuine products. Whatever the real reason, the price of legitimate DVDs in video stores crashed and most went out of business, so nowadays you find major Hollywood films on the shelf at your local pound shop. Who needs a legitimate DVD that will only be watched a few times, for ten pounds, if they can buy three that have just hit the cinemas, from a dodgy looking fella for a few quid? Things have changed with people being able to download and stream, but there are still crooks marketing counterfeit versions.

And where do I fit into all of this you may be asking yourself? Well as you know I wasn't a big-time crook, especially no crime boss. I was a mindless thug, a dumb and greedy street thief at the bottom of the criminal food chain. So, there I was at a bus stop, minding my own business, looking out for the police, when I was approached and offered DVDs. How could I refuse? I was broke and desperate after Gordon disappeared, so I lured the seller around the back of a garage and started to look through his bag. Then I politely told him they were mine, but it seemed the only word he knew in English was 'DVD.' As I made to move away I guessed he was weak so after that I'd no intention of handing back his bag. I whacked him over the head with it, splitting the bottom in the process. As hundred or so DVDs spread across the floor I managed to grab half of them, ran off and sold the lot for 30 quid to some geezers in a cab office. I must say I was chuffed with myself.

In a narrow-minded way, I genuinely thought there was nothing wrong with what I'd done. My victim was probably an illegal immigrant and a criminal on my streets. In truth, I was a greedy bully and he, like others I stole from, were soft targets. 'I've found an easy way to make money,' I thought to myself.

I started to come across these sellers all the time, like a magnet I just pulled them in. You had to know where to look but being mostly foreigners they were not hard to spot. They looked lost, you could tell they weren't locals, some had only been in the country for a few days then had been forced to go out selling. I'd see them walking from shop-to-shop looking confused, carrying a hold-all, rucksack or large carrier bag from Sainsburys. It would give me a little buzz when I spotted them. Sometimes I got it wrong, and I'd approach someone asking to buy DVDs, only for him to say he didn't sell them. Still not convinced I'd go through his bag to find vegetables or tools. I didn't bother to apologise, I was just pissed-off. Yes. I know, I was one horrible bastard. I'd head out on trains or buses hunting these sellers. If the poor guys returned to base empty handed they'd probably be punished by their slave masters, so not all of them handed stuff over without a fight.

One day I noticed a seller alongside a train station and politely asked, 'Any DVDs?' A good tactic was to wave a five-pound note in the man's face when, even though intimidated by my looks, the need for money took over his mind. We'd find a quiet location where I could look at what he had. Sometimes I was too cocky like when I had a seller down an ally, grabbed his bag and a tug-of-war started. I'd been beaten with many weapons over the years, so resistance didn't faze me. Each day I'd be at it again. I was so confident I once robbed three in one day.

It was a bonus if you managed to steal their money as well, but this rarely happened. The most I ever got from a single victim was around £100. I'd brag to pub customers about how I came to own my bag of DVDs and they would joke about how one day I'd end up robbing the wrong man, a Bruce Lee-type who'd fight back. That's exactly what happened. As I sat on the bus, I noticed this young Chinese guy a few seats in front, my radar didn't start ringing as I initially thought he was a student. But on closer inspection I was certain I could make out the shape of DVDs in his luggage. I followed him off the bus to see him walk down an alley, certain in my mind he was off to sell films.

I shadowed his movements until the bus was out of sight. With his head-phones on, he never heard me approaching him. I tried to grab the bag from him and in shock he spun round and went into a fight mode. With that we set about each other. It wasn't exactly Bruce Lee versus Chuck Norris from 'Way of the Dragon,' more South London thug against 18-year-old karate expert. With lighting speed, I received a kick to the side of my head, knocking me into reality. This was no longer a simple DVD raid it was a proper fight. I put my fists up and protected myself from another kick to the head. I threw two or three punches missing my target by far, and with that came his third kick which I blocked with my fists, but I also grabbed his leg. His shoe came off. And as I swung him around he lost balance and fell to the floor. I started to punch him in the face and he kicked-out.

My lip was bleeding and I thought 'Fuck this.' I started to walk off leaving the man on the floor. All of a sudden I felt an almighty pain in the back of my neck and with that fell to the floor as he unleashed more punches to my head and body. As he tried to run off I grabbed a lump of wood lying on the grass and started chasing him. The bastard was fast, but I whacked him around the legs. Can you believe it, he still came at me punching and kicking? In the process his bag finally fell to the floor and with me swinging the piece of wood at him he finally backed-off as I grabbed the prize. I spat the blood from my mouth and made my exit, the DVDs making-up for my wounds.

Next day was spent selling five for a tenner. I'd walk into barbers, pubs and offices. I'd sold so many I became known as 'The DVD Man.' I'd go into the local hairdressers and a staff member would shout out, 'The DVD man's here if anyone wants any.' None of my customers knew how I got hold of the goods, maybe they thought I had a tame wholesaler somewhere!

Whilst I was in Kentucky Fried Chicken eating a Zinger Tower Burger for lunch and reading the paper, out of the corner of my eye I noticed a guy tucking into some Popcorn Chicken. I thought, 'Oh damn, it's another seller on my patch.' I was tired but in my warped state of mind rules were rules, and it was my duty to sort out this guy. I'd become so brazen that I just walked up to him in front of a crowd of customers and snatched his bag. He tried to grab it back, so I kicked him hard forcing him back into his seat.

A week or so later I was in a café when I noticed a man looking through the window. It was the same one I'd robbed in KFC. He was fuming and banged on the window to try and scare me. Now if I'd run away, he'd have had the upper hand, so I jumped from my seat and chased him down the road. When I returned to the café, I overheard the customers talking about how I was the main man and that I controlled the whole thing. In my foolish mind I relished the thought and walked off with a bit of a stride, pushing my chest out!

Some of the DVDs I came across were weird or disgusting, but I guess with piracy being an illegal trade most sellers didn't care what they pushed. I came across strange movies and some of the titles would make you cringe. There was porn, gay porn, transsexual porn, fake 'snuff movies' and animal porn, disturbing to say the least. I'm glad to say I never did sell anyone a copy of the last of these though for a laugh I once replaced normal porn with some transsexual stuff and sold it to one sucker. He didn't complain when I returned a week later. He must have enjoyed it.

Was I dangerous? Yes I was. Being in prison had made me a whole lot more violent. Was I arrogant and cocky? Yes I was. For all the shit that had happened to me in my fucked-up life I was very, very angry. I thought the world owed me something for my pain. I took out my anger on the DVD sellers; I bullied them as I knew they were weaker and scared living in a strange country all alone. Do I regret my actions? Yes! But at the time I felt they were criminals too, and there's no honour amongst thieves.

London is a dangerous place altogether, it has a murky underworld, with many levels of criminality, from the counterfeit DVD seller to the street robber, armed robber, drug dealer, arms dealer and drug baron, all the way up to organized crime boss. Hundreds of different types of crime and criminals, with an unofficial class system within the criminal community. Nearly everyone hates sex offenders, or those who've killed women and children. 'I'm just a violent counterfeit DVD seller and I often receive beatings in return,' I consoled myself.

CHAPTER 11

Familiar Walls

I remember sitting in a greasy spoon around the corner from my hideout waiting for Sarah. I hadn't seen her since her miscarriage. I'd been dealing with the loss of that baby and splitting-up with her the only way I knew how, through violence. She noticed my new clothes and the pathetic gold earring. I thought I was cool, with a few pounds to spend. In reality this was my way of showing her I didn't need her, and that I definitely didn't need her father's handouts. A normal man would have grafted hard to prove he'd the strength to stand on his own feet, but I was not normal and hadn't been coping well. I hadn't spoken to anyone in my family in weeks, I just mixed with the street criminals and nut jobs I met around the Big Smoke.

The police had calmed down their search for me at her parents' address, believing their pleas: 'Leave us alone, we haven't seen him for weeks.' We started our relationship once again, but this time around she rarely visited my hideaway as she felt uncomfortable in that grimy environment. Our time together blossomed as much as it could then it came abruptly to an end.

Never trust a crackhead. A week or so before my arrest I'd given the crack addict who lived downstairs a bag of DVDs to sell for me. I found out that he'd sold them on for crack. I learned never, ever to trust someone with a crack habit, they'll steal from their closest friends, even their own mother. It is a despicable drug causing misery across the UK and throughout the world. If you took every single gram of crack off our streets crimes like shoplifting, car thefts and domestic break-ins would fall dramatically.

So now the crack fiend was on a come down regretting what he'd done, wondering how he could come home knowing I'd be waiting there for him.

Then the slippery character got wind I was on the run, and it doesn't take a genius to see how he got out of his current issue. Faster than the speed of light he dialed 999. Whatever happened to love thy neighbour? In his world it was rob thy neighbour.

I stepped out of my flat with a strange feeling in my stomach, I knew something was up. As I headed into the main road I noticed a police car parked opposite with two cops in it, staring at me. I went with my instinct and headed back home with my door key in my sweaty palm. I was three steps from freedom when I heard another car screech to a halt. It was the CID, and as I made for the entrance a woman officer screamed, 'Grab him ... Justin Rollins we're arresting you for possession of an imitation firearm and robbery.'

Sitting in the back of the police car I realised the crackhead must have grassed my whereabouts. Back at the police station I was slung into a cell. I was gutted to say the least at losing everything and I lay there feeling completely useless and sorry for myself. I was letting out silent screams, I hated being locked-up and I hated my life.

With that I ripped-off my T-shirt, tied it around my neck and started to strangle myself. Just like old times. But this was more of a cry for help as I knew the police would probably see me on the in-cell CCTV and soon rush to save me. But I was reckless, what if they'd not seen me, I could have choked to death. Of course, a minute or so later they entered my cell. They stripped me naked, then threw me a white paper suit. I was told my cell door would remain open as I was not to be trusted.

I can't say that I slept well under observation in that stinky holding cell and first thing in the morning I was stuffed dazed and bleary-eyed into a sweat box heading to Wimbledon Magistrates' Court. I remember sitting there for the short drive staring through the one-way glass at normal members of society heading off to work. Deep down I wished I was joining their rat race but in stead I was locked-up like an animal.

'What's the point of even going to court?' I thought. I knew I'd be remanded in custody until the next hearing. I was told by the magistrate that I'd be on my way to Wandsworth Prison shortly and my next court appearance would be in a month's time. Wandsworth is known by cons as 'Wanno.' It has a reputation as a hard place and I truly dreaded going there. Already I was worrying about picking-up my old prison paranoia and OCD. If I'd never suffered with these issues then I reckon I could have served my time easily back then.

This jail was full of career criminals, proper gangsters and one too many addicts. As I entered the holding cell, I noticed some of my old enemies' names on the wall amongst the graffiti, so I knew I had to be on my guard. Wandsworth was bursting at the seams with prisoners; it was three inmates to a double cell and two to a single. This type of bang up is unbearable during a hot summer and with only an hour out to exercise each day. There were fights regularly.

The next day I wandered round the exercise yard looking at the different types of prisoners, white geezers, black gangsters, Muslims and so on. While scanning the black prisoners, I recognised a face, and as I got closer I heard the voice. 'Oh my God,' I thought and shouted out, 'G … G … G … ' With that Gordon turned towards me and our faces lit-up as we rushed to make an embracing man hug. Shit, being in such a dark place it was so good to see a friendly face.

Back on the prison unit we asked the officers if we could be put in a cell together and our request was granted. It was just like the time back at our flat in South London. He asked what happened to Bella and he wasn't impressed when I told him I'd sold her. I said I wasn't impressed with him leaving me like he did. He then explained what had happened. He told me that he and a couple of associates had found out the address of a suspected cannabis factory. One of his associates owned a trained pit bull and the plan was to kick the door off, push the pit bull in and it would attack these strangers as it was trained to do. G and his friends would then barge in, put the dog on the lead, and bag up the plants. But from the beginning all hell broke loose. After breaking the door down and pushing the dog through it they were met by a scared man. The dog had him cornered in the kitchen as G and his friends ran through the house with their heavy duty bags. They found the room with the cannabis in it and started chopping down the plants and filling their bags to the sound of the dog barking in the background.

After a few minutes they couldn't hear the dog anymore and were concentrating on stealing the cannabis. As they started to make their exit, to their horror they noticed the dog lying in a pool of blood. G's friend was in shock, but they had to leave because the police had been called. His associates left before he did and a Vietnamese man with a knife jumped out and stabbed G in the arm. He did this using the knife he'd just used to kill the dog. G dropped his bag of plants and ran from the house in pain. They all made it back to the car and G drove off, his arm pouring with blood.

G's driving was erratic and caught the attention of the police, then after he failed to stop they gave chase. The plan to lose them was that G's two friends would jump out when he suddenly stopped and run-off in the hope the police would stop chasing the car. It didn't work because after they did so the police carried on chasing G and he was arrested. Whilst he was receiving stitches for an arm wound they found the bags of cannabis and a knife belonging to one of the friends. G was arrested for driving while disqualified and possession of a large amount of cannabis plus an offensive weapon. His friends were never caught. The Vietnamese growers never phoned the police as they would have been arrested as well. G reckoned that he was looking at a year inside or maybe longer, although he was hoping for a community order. He was to be sentenced in a couple of weeks' time. Saying goodbye to my friend again was a hard thing. I was gutted but wished him well.

As I lay on my bunk with my court sentencing appearance looming, I had a thought that I believed was pure genius. I remembered the report my psychologist Rachel had written before I was released from Aylesbury Prison. This clearly stated that I should receive ongoing mental health support. Did I get it, no I did not! 'This could be my ticket to freedom,' I told myself. When the doors were unlocked, I quickly headed for the phone to ring my Mum. I urged her to get onto Aylesbury and speak to Rachel telling her of my current situation and to see if she could send my solicitor a copy. A couple of days later she told me that Rachel was upset I hadn't received any treatment at all upon release and that she would send the report straightaway.

I remember waiting in a holding cell ready for my court appearance when a couple of cons asked what I was up for. When I replied possession of an imitation firearm they reckoned I'd get three to five years. I didn't know it at the time, but I couldn't have received a sentence that high as the maximum you could get in a magistrates' court was far less. But their opinion only worsened my nerves and to make matters worse it was the morning of my sister's wedding and I was gutted I'd not be attending it. My future brother-in-law was even going to turn up at court before their marriage to plead for my release.

I sat behind a glass screen with my fingers crossed hoping for the best. My solicitor got up and spoke of how I should not even be sentenced on this date as further mental health reports were needed. Also that I should not be incarcerated as upon release from my last sentence I was not given the support I needed. The court retired for the magistrates to read Rachel's report. From what I was told were legal reasons, I've never been allowed to see her full report, even though it was written about me. But whatever it said the judges went along with it and by an extreme stroke of luck, or an act of God, I was released from the court I'd run out of seven months earlier and I was given bail pending further reports. The chair of the court even looked at me and said, 'You better get ready for the ball, you've a wedding to attend.'

So, after six months on the run and a month in Wanno I was back on the streets. During those years as a criminal, I suffered some unlucky times, but they were often balanced by times like that. After signing some paperwork, I jumped into my brother-in-law to be's car and we headed for the wedding! What a buzz, from Wandsworth Prison to Wimbledon, to quickly putting on a suit and giving my sister away on her big day. I remember the sun was blazing. Looking back though, in the wedding photos you can clearly see my prison pallor and that I'd lost a lot of weight. Being on the run isn't being free; it's a nervy time knowing you can lose everything at the drop of a hat. I wasn't exactly some major criminal that could afford plastic surgery and head to the Costa Del Sol. I was a petty thug.

Things seemed brighter at last; it was looking like I'd receive some sort of mental health support and a community sentence when I headed back at court. For once in my life, I felt I could make a change and turn my back on the old me. I wasn't a fool. A new road would not be easy. I knew there would be many challenges. It was now time to grit my teeth and try to find my place in normal society. Maybe this time around I could stay out of trouble...

CHAPTER 12

Back on the Road

On my release I moved into Sarah's parents' house. Her father went out of his way to try and see me on the straight and narrow. He even got me my first real job through a friend, as a painter and decorator. Can you believe it I was 22 and about to start my first proper job? I was nervous, of course, what with that first day in this new world, but I puffed-out my chest and headed-off to join normal society.

I was working right opposite New Scotland Yard, up mountains of scaffolding, scraping-off the old paint from office windows. Very aware of my fellow workers in my usual hypervigilant state I was cautious about them. But they were mostly ex-convicts so somehow I fitted-in. Some things hadn't changed though. I'd bunk the train from Carshalton to Victoria each day, and run through the ticket barrier behind some businessman heading for the City. 'Just a bit of fare evasion,' I thought, 'whilst I'm trying to sort myself out.' One thing that left me feeling anxious was when my workmates spotted the scars on my wrists, then I was paranoid about what they thought of me.

I know some people say who cares but try sitting in a nice restaurant with gashes all over your arms, people stare at you like you're some sort of freak. I guess when I was in that self-harming realm in prison I *was* a freak. There it was normal to walk around covered in wounds. But in the civilised world I was self-conscious of my scars. I knew full well I wasn't what you'd call normal, I'd been through a lot of deep, dark trauma and was not yet ready to deal with my past. So, heading off to work I tried to find my place but underneath I was still angry and disturbed. I only lasted a week. I found it difficult to cope, to hold down a conversation. I questioned myself, my thoughts, and their words. I was always thinking something bad. Was I not funny? Didn't they like me? What did he say? These constant worries drained me. Thinking of yourself as a freak and living in fight or flight mode is mentally exhausting, I'd wake-up in the morning with stress and headaches. Then I got sacked for not going into work.

I couldn't explain the reason for losing my job to Gerry my probation officer even though this one turned out to be a decent guy. Though hard and strict he was fair. But I'd heard that if you took the piss he'd send you straight back to prison. He wrote me a wicked pre-sentence report for my upcoming court appearance concerning the firearms offence. It recommended I serve a supervision order with him as long as there was mental health support. Gerry's report, which sat alongside Rachel's from Aylesbury, did the trick. I received a long probation order and had to attend sessions with a local psychiatrist.

Gerry informed me that I was under the close eye of MAPPA, which stands for Multi Agency Public Protection Arrangements. MAPPA was made up of different authorities managing dangerous criminals in the community, armed robbers, sex offenders, violent offenders, and those with some sort of mental-illness or personality disorder. The authorities involved were the National Probation Service, HM Prison Service and the police. They shared intelligence and got together for meetings.

There were three categories: Category 1 for registered sex offenders (RSOs); Category 2 for offenders who received a custodial sentence of 12 months or for a sexual or violent offence; and Category 3 for anyone who posed a 'risk of serious harm to the public,' etc. I was placed in Category 3 due to my CPTSD and history of violence. The question was 'Why would somebody with my background be carrying an air weapon in public?'

As well as these categories there are three different levels you could be placed on: Level One, which represents the normal inter-agency management of an offender in the community by one agency but with some liaison; Level Two where MAPPA meetings are held when the offender's management is discussed between the various parties involved in their case; and Level Three, essentially the same as Level Two, except that senior management attend and greater resources are expected to be used. Those in Level Three are sometimes called 'the critical few,' offenders posing the highest level of risk and who normally need a strategically coordinated risk management plan, predatory sex offenders, arsonists, extremely violent offenders, dangerous mentally-ill offenders, terrorists or people with dangerous personality disorders. At MAPPA meetings the agencies share confidential information and often adopt a pro-active strategy. I was placed on Level 2 and told the police would keep tabs on me, follow my movements and put me under close surveillance if my risk level happened to rise. Gerry said not to be alarmed if I got a knock on the door by plain clothes officers asking how I was doing.

'What the hell, doesn't he know I'm still paranoid?' I asked myself. From the day he told me I might be followed my hypervigilance was extreme. I looked-out of the window scanning for unmarked cars, I was alert to every sound. I remember a man sitting outside my mother's house in a car occasionally looking towards her house. I was convinced I was being watched. When I told Gerry he just told me to relax. To this day I don't know if it was MAPPA officers or someone else following me, but it freaked me out. I'd already got rid of one stalker and now I felt as if it was happening again.

Gerry would go on about how he disliked the fact that when a crime had been committed it was no longer about the victim but the 'poor offender from a shit background' and so on. I'd think, 'What's this guy going on about?' Looking back, he was right and he did teach me a few things; most criminals went on probation looking for sympathy, not giving a damn about their victims. In reality, the criminal, no matter how 'hard done by' they think they are has *no right to go out hurting people.*

Gerry started to make me think a bit differently and urged me to stand on my own feet. He asked how I felt about him getting me my own place by him talking to the council. Of course, I was well-impressed when a few weeks later he said they were offering me a flat. It was on an estate I knew quite well. I remember visiting it and seeing it was boarded-up.

My panic set in, seeing the landings and knowing the area was crime ridden. The idea that this would be my new home took me straight back to Aylesbury. My chest hurt with fear as I saw each flat in the block as a cell. In my eyes the locals going about their business were prisoners on the unit. I was in a state of terror and tormented, because fear of this kind was normal to me. I lived with these thoughts every day. Even if you'd put me in a beautiful, detached house in a totally safe environment my mind would still have been with me, I never believed I was safe.

After explaining to Gerry that this was not a healthy environment and it could up my level of risk, he battled with the council and after they'd ummed and ahhhd they found me a maisonette somewhere else. Can you believe it, I now finally had a place I could call home, I'd no longer have to stay at other people's houses and memories of sleeping rough would be far away in the back of my mind? Anybody could have a house, but now I had a home, and your home is your security, your resting place.

I moved in quickly and since I barely had any money Gerry got me a grant to buy things like a washing machine, fridge and cooker. I asked Sarah to move in with me and had a spring in my step believing I was at last onto better things. Her parents were not at their happiest though, losing their youngest child, but we were only down the road from them, so they still saw her every day.

I remember the little things like doing our first food shop together, the amount of crap we bought. But we were happy in our new home eating shit food. To our left was an old lady called Ivy, above her a guy called Tony, who owned a three-wheeler. Straight above there lived a middle-aged man with mental-health problems. I remember getting my first letter and opening it proudly, only to find out that it was an ASBO warning. 'What the fuck?' I thought. It was the mad guy that lived above, complaining of noise. Believe me I was a quiet bastard in my own home and if I'd made a noise why didn't he just knock and ask me politely to keep it down. 'The fucking grass,' I thought.

I knocked on his door and asked why he'd made up such things and his response was that I shouldn't even be at that address, further that I was 'the live in boyfriend' staying secretly with Sarah whose place it really was. After showing him the ASBO letter and calling him a wanker, he slammed the door in my face.

Nowadays I can understand what noise can do to someone with mental-health issues. If you're in a bad state, you don't want it. Sounds that most people don't even notice, someone in a hypervigilant frame of mind will hear and hear loudly. When you're constantly traumatised by your own thoughts and then you pick up on noises you can have a meltdown. This neighbour quickly moved out and I believe he was sectioned under the Mental Health Act.

The other neighbours were as good as gold, and I'd help out the old boy, Tony when feral kids would up tip his three-wheeler for a laugh. They were giving him the V-sign as he tried to stop them, but I'd chase them down the road. Going back to my teens, I was one of those kids and would have thought it hilarious to overturn someone's lightweight car so I kind of understood, but I was also learning fast that this kind of behaviour is completely wrong.

Sarah started to settle into 'our' new home. It wasn't long before she fell pregnant again and this time the pregnancy went smoothly. I was about to become a father for the first time...

Mental Me

CHAPTER 13

Fatherhood

W as I ready to become a dad? Was I at all ready to look after a child, giving it stability and guidance? After years of a crazy rollercoaster ride of self-destruction no I wasn't. Yes, I'd made small changes to my lifestyle and cut out a lot of negative things, but I wasn't cured of my issues. We thought we knew better than Sarah's parents and my Mum, we thought we could handle looking after a small child, but how wrong could we be? We barely knew how to look after ourselves and, looking back, our relationship wasn't the healthiest. We had become inseparable but not in a 'lovey dovey' kind of way, it was in an insecure way.

For two people to be together twenty-four-seven and neither of them with a life outside of that environment is always going to be a recipe for disaster. But back then we were too needy of each other and clingy. I'd never had a proper relationship before and neither of us knew the basics to make it work. Confined to the maisonette most of the time we started to feel like crap. We didn't go out mixing or to social events, at that stage everyone was still a threat to me, I hardly trusted anyone, so why would I be socialising? I'd never been shown love in my childhood, so how could I show love to anyone else, furthermore how could I accept love. I was suspicious of everyone, to my mind they all had an ulterior motive. I couldn't get my head around people being nice. They were not to be trusted. I was like a wounded animal struggling for survival.

As Sarah's bump started to get bigger I never appreciated the strain she was under, never knew how she felt with her body changing and why on some days she felt ugly. If my body was in great shape and then over a period of nine months it started changing and stretching, I think I wouldn't be the happiest person either, but back then I was too unwise and selfish to care for her needs. I didn't even acknowledge the changes that were happening. It's only looking back now that I can see I needed to man-up and take responsibility.

The nine months of Sarah's pregnancy passed quickly and in April she suddenly went into labour; I remember holding her hand giving her words of encouragement. She just screamed at me. At the hospital Sarah pushed and pushed and believed she was doing well. I could see this mop of thick black hair starting to come out, it was scary as hell. Then the doctor produced an assisted delivery suction cup and stuck it onto the bit of my child's head that was showing. I didn't know what to do. I thought, 'Do I punch the doctor or let her do it?' I didn't know what was going on. The doctor pulled so hard next thing you know she was lying on her back on the floor with medical equipment scattered everywhere.

Most probably out of stress the baby started to go to the toilet inside Sarah, and that was it, the doctor was back on her feet armed with a pair of scissors. She cut Sarah open enough to pull our child out, and with that blood and baby poo went everywhere. It was like a scene from 'The Exorcist' but ten times worse. The child stopped breathing for a while so she was put in an incubator. The whole thing was too much for me and I burst into tears. The tears felt weird I must say, why wasn't I angry, why wasn't I in pain? Were they actually tears of joy?! I'd only ever felt tears of stress and strain before these. They felt so clean as they poured down my face.

I left the room and got on the phone to my mother and she tells me she didn't understand a word as I cried and mumbled rubbish to her. Can you believe it I was a dad with a beautiful daughter. We named her Gabriella. I went back into the delivery room and just stared at this baby, still in an incubator, her eyes were open and taking her first look at the world. The doctor asked me If I'd like to hold her but I just froze. The tears started to fall once again, and it dawned on me that our child was pure, clean and innocent and I felt dirty. I was covered in tattoos of the Grim Reaper and torn hearts. My face, head and body were full of scars from prison and street battles. My energy felt dark and unclean, I was ashamed and didn't feel good enough to pick up my own child. She looked like an angel and there I was, this man who'd rolled with killers and robbers, staring down at something so delicate and beautiful. I was nasty and screwed-up and felt bad for bringing her into a world I saw as hell. When

I finally did get the guts to pick up Gabriella and hold her my tears kept falling. The rest of the day was a blur.

Can you believe I could fight and use weapons, I could self-harm and set fire to my prison cell, but I found it so hard just to cradle my child? That needed great effort. It was a wonderful but at the same time strange day. I didn't know how much my daughter would change my life, the way I viewed the world. I never thought a tiny little baby could really make changes in me. But bless my little angel she did, and massive ones too. So there we are hey, my little girl changed my life, I turned over a new leaf and we all lived happily ever after, I can end my book here and we can all go to bed!

Come on, things were never going to be that easy-peasy lemon squeezy. Remember I was still not over my messed-up, fucked-up, screwed-up past! I was becoming a man, but deep down I was still just a boy. But for now I thought life would be great once me and Sarah got our baby back home. I swear, the first night there Gabriella screamed the house down. We were completely drained from the past two days, but the constant crying made it even worse. 'Why won't she just shut up?' I asked Sarah. She didn't know what to do. It was an eye-opener. There and then in our tired, emotionally drained state we both knew parenting wasn't going to be a walk in the park.

I was so tired and moody I got Sarah to phone her parents and they picked-up her and Gabriella at three in the morning. Being the selfish prick I was I fell into a nice, deep sleep. For around seven to eight hours I was at peace, no baby, no screaming, no stressed-out baby's mother around. No responsibility, back then neither of us could handle responsibility in any sense of the word.

Sarah and Gabriella came back next day and the screaming continued. I didn't realise that the more tired we got the more would Gabriella. She got up every night to feed Gabriella whilst I lay in bed. I tried to ignore that this was making her feel even more drained, bad about herself, or that a baby needed a calm, loving environment. With my PTSD mood swings I couldn't give her or the baby the right support. Some days I'd sit there holding Gabriella, pretending to myself that I loved being a father, but in truth I just saw a screaming child that had ruined our lovely, stable relationship.

Yeah, I know, what stable relationship? When you have PTSD there is zero stability! Boy, was I mad? It feels strange looking back and to talk of Gabriella in this way. I do remember the few times I'd take her out on my own, which were kind of bonding sessions however poor. I'd wrap her up nice and warm put her in her buggy and walk for miles. Sometimes we went out and did family things, I remember we took her to Hampton Court for the day for a picnic and made loads of photos. From the outside Sarah's parents probably thought we'd turned a corner, but when we were back at home the arguments would start all over again.

I'd feel quite vulnerable walking around with Gabriella too, with a past like mine who could tell when an old enemy might creep-up on the attack? If you've lived a life of crime, gangs and violence it is always worrying bringing a child into this crazy world. After one of our more positive days out as a family we pulled-up outside our home and I started to take the shopping in whilst Sarah got Gabriella out of the car. I noticed a neighbour who lived over the road outside in his car with a passenger. As I took the shopping into the kitchen, I could hear a horn being pressed over-and-over again. I knew straightaway what they were doing, they knew it too. They knew who I was, of my reputation and they wanted to test me. They were trying to get Sarah's attention as well as she tried to lift Gabriella out of our car without waking her up.

I went to help as the neighbour started pressing the horn louder and louder. I looked towards them with an evil glare as I held Gabriella in her car seat. 'BIB! BIB! BIB! I looked over again and saw the young passenger, a teenager, in the back of the car who got out and screamed, 'Whats your fucking problem, Paki … We're not bibbing at you.' With that he ran across the busy road and squared-up into my face saying, 'You want it, you fucking Paki?' In all my life I'd never been so disrespected, and this was happening with my newborn baby in my arms. 'This child is half me,' I thought, 'so he's calling her a Paki too!' Gabriella had now woken-up to a scene of aggressive, racist screaming in her father's face, taunting him to fight. The scene got out of hand and other neighbours came out to see what was going on. All around me was a blur as I heard nothing but shouting, Gabriella crying and Sarah screaming.

I snapped out of the blur and saw red. I threw the shopping on the floor and in a weird moment where everything seemed to stand still I remember the bag ripping and a carton of orange juice and a tin of beans go rolling down across a patch of grass into the road. I don't even remember putting Gabriella down, but the next thing I know I was back in our kitchen slipping a kitchen knife up my sleeve. I then ran back out of the house and into the boy's face asking, 'You want it, you cunt?' He put up his fists and I pulled out the knife to sounds of utter disbelief from the gathering crowd. I just loved seeing his smirking face drop and fear overtake him. What followed was a true cat-and-mouse chase as this young bully darted around Sarah's car with me after him. It was like a scene from a cartoon as we ran in circles and I tried to stab him. He was laughing to impress his friends, but his cowardly giggles soon turned to cries for help. I've played out the scene many times in my head. What if he'd tripped? What if I'd caught him? I was full of rage. 'My child ... my daughter, and Sarah ... he's scared them and that's enough to make any man flip,' I thought. I'm glad I never did catch him, or I'd surely be banged-up in prison serving a very long sentence rather than writing this. I'm lucky as my life may have turned out differently, and I'm also grateful to the person, I don't know who, who came over and took the knife away.

'What fracas, it never happened?' seemed to be the question in everybody's mind when the police showed-up in numbers. Those in the street told them that it was just 'a tiny scuffle' with no mention of a weapon. I couldn't believe that they backed me, it seems they saw through my actions and realised I'd been provoked. The neighbour who started it all came to apologise, saying he was sorry for his young friend's actions. But in my mind I knew it was bullshit; if he was sorry, why would he have let the friend out of the car in the first place. I'd seen the bully involved in the weeks leading up to the incident and every time I'd been met with an evil stare. He was just out to make a name for himself. If he'd taken me out he would have felt like the big bad boy, but who would do such a thing?! Because of this coward Sarah was too scared to stay at home as we feared he might seek revenge. I remember that first night I got a friend to bring me a sword in case he paid a visit.

This enemy didn't come again and though I have had many terrible things done to me, and I'm not an innocent because I have also dished out a lot of dirt, I will never forget what he did that day! I have forgiven many bad people from my past life but for some reason I find it difficult get over this event. Yeah, if you have an issue confront me or approach me when I'm on my own not when I'm in the company of my innocent child.

For the first time I started to go out to clubs and bars with friends. I'd never done things like this before because of the years spent in prison. It gave me a small sense of feeling good about myself, the way I dressed, the girls I seemed to be attracting. As I danced, I had the odd flash of Gabriella and Sarah deep within my mind, but as my friends ordered another round those thoughts faded quickly. What I was doing was clear to see, I was 22 and catching-up, running away from responsibility like a lot of young (and older) men do. My father did it to me, was I going to turn out like him? For now, all I could hear was the loud bass from the sound system, I could no longer hear the cries of my daughter.

In the mornings, after clubbing, feeling hungover with my ears still ringing, I felt guilty as my thoughts turned to our little family. Sarah had now rented her own flat from the council as we thought this would give us more space and make the arguments less frequent. But still being stalked by Jimmy Walker, she found it extremely hard to be alone. To make up for the selfish man that I'd become I started to do up her new flat. I got her a sofa and a TV, as well as helping her to move in. We spent more time together and I'd take her out for a meal or treat her and Gabriella. This small phase of us trying to make things work went on for around three weeks. Then one day Sarah asked me to look after Gabriella for the day whilst she went to the gym and had some time to herself. That's when I felt a kick to the stomach as I got news from one of her friends that she was not at the gym and in fact was with another man. I was at my sister's when I heard this and was hurt by the fact that she was probably right then at her new flat with him.

It dawned on me that I'd spent time and money doing up Sarah's flat and though she felt too scared to stay there on her own she was using it as a secret rendezvous for her and another guy. I'd thought we were making a go of things, but in reality the last few weeks now meant nothing and I was hurting like hell. I asked my sister to look after Gabriella, grabbed a screwdriver and headed over towards Sarah's shagging den. Once again, I am glad I never caught the guy as I know I'd have done something bad to him.

I tried kicking in the door but got no answer. I then left in a near psychotic mood, overcome with anger and pain. I rushed back to my sister's place and swore to her that I was keeping my child. But what right did I have, and I was known for violence, so if the police turned-up they would take my child from me in seconds? Phone calls went back and forth between Sarah and me as she cried for and demanded her daughter and I screamed that she was mine. I sat on my sister's sofa holding the poor child, she didn't deserve to be brought into my fucked-up world, and I cried to the little angel, 'I'm sorry sweet girl for this mess, I really am.' Then I just sat and sobbed to her.

There was a loud bang at the door. My sister was confronted by Sarah's mum as she insisted on having Gabriella back. She told me Sarah wouldn't have done such a thing with another man, and this made me even more angry as Sarah had already admitted it to me. All this made me feel helpless and desperate. I screamed at my sister not to hand Gabriella over, but Sarah's mother swore back saying that she would phone the police. A tug-of-war started. Everyone was crying and after Sarah's mother begged, 'Please let her come with me, I'm like her mum, I have been raising her' my sister let go. It dawned on me that I'd hardly bonded with my child over the six months she'd been in this world. But it hurt like hell.

The thought of being helpless and somebody taking my child away from me was such a terrible feeling. I begged Sarah's mother to let me see Gabriella again and she promised I could. But for now, my 'Lil Bubba' was gone. The incident made me feel that the mother always has far more rights, and though I'm allowed to see Gabriella wherever or whenever, I have always told myself that if her mother tried to stop this I'd join Fathers for Justice, scale buildings and invade high-profile events to fight for my rights!

Why all of this anger, stress and pain? Why wouldn't it just go away? Why couldn't someone just knock some bloody sense into me for once? That is exactly what happened. It took getting my head kicked in like a punctured football and for me to be up on fresh charges that carried a sentence of life imprisonment for me to finally turn the corner. To change negatives into positives. The incident had such an impact on me it altered my life once and for all ... and eventually for the better.

CHAPTER 14

The Night a DJ Saved My Life

I didn't have contact with Sarah for two months after the latest drama; I was hurting inside and I felt cheated. Did I deserve it? Back then I did, and I hit the self-destruct button again. For a while I was like Sister Sledge, lost in the music as I hit the clubs and drank hard. I'd always had an issue with alcohol; put it this way mixing it with PTSD is a bit like throwing a match onto petrol. I was off my bloody nut. I'd drive at 60 miles an hour through red lights and get a sick buzz from taking a risk. When I drank, I was out-of-control ... and I'd been drinking from a young age.

I entered my local LOVE-2-LOVE not having any idea of the trouble that lay ahead in the club. The drinks were flowing like a drum and bass MC on speed and I got lost in the night and inside my mind. Then I headed to the toilets and looked at myself in the mirror. A man pissing in the urinal shouted, 'Oi mate, you a Muslim?' I stared in the mirror seeing the blackness in my eyes and my old prison glare looking back at me. Filled with aggression I ripped my shirt down my chest and with the Grim Reaper visible on one side, a heartless sign on the other, and various other sick tattoos on display, I screamed back, 'Do I look like a fucking Muslim?'

Lucifer was back in town and feeling charged with hatred and evil I left and went back to the dancing. The next couple of hours are a blur, but I know for certain I was in a foul mood as the drink messed with my already fucked-up mind. Me and a friend left the club around 2.30 am. It was Bank Holiday and the streets filled with drunken geezers and ladies freezing in their miniskirts. Welcome to Binge Britain, screaming, shouting, some bird being sick over her mate, another ripping her best friend's hair out, a guy taking a piss and flashing his dick at passers-by. Police were standing around looking out for trouble, the taxi men were trying for customers.

We sat in the car drunk as skunks, blasting loud music, still in party mood. I started the engine and drove five minutes down the road, but something wouldn't let either of us go, I'm sure the word is 'FATE.' My hands turned the steering wheel and we headed back. We parked up and stood with the rest of the crowds not anticipating what was about to happen. There was a large group of men across the road shouting abuse in my direction. Not to be a spoilsport I shouted back, and with that the one with probably the smallest rep decided to stand in the middle of the road and offer me out. He'd a lot of mates with him and must have thought I'd back down. Being the fool I was and on my own turf I refused to do that. I jumped the railings between us and got in the guy's face and as he punched me I fell back, then I hit him square on the nose bursting it like a balloon.

What seemed like a swarm of locusts was soon onto me. I felt these hungry wolves come at me throwing punches as I swung my fists trying to fight back. But they overwhelmed me. I put my hand in my pocket and pulled out my car keys, my only tool to defend myself. I pushed a key hard into my attacker's cheek, pulling it down as much as I could. As I got pushed against a wall, which most probably saved my life as it helped me to stay on my feet, I dropped the keys. There was no defending myself now. All I could do was cover my head with my arms and pray for the attack to stop.

The CCTV clearly showed them attacking me, and with my shirt now ripped clean off and my jeans around my ankles I was near enough naked as I got savagely beaten with fists, bottles and kicks. There wasn't room for a whole gang to hit me but each of them had a go in turn. I remember hearing a voice in my head echoing, 'Please stop, please stop, it wasn't meant to go on this long!' Can you believe it that even after taking so many hidings over the years, in my crazy mind I thought there was a time limit to the attack! The police just stood there watching, too intimidated to help me. Funny how, when you really need them they can be useless. Everyone just stood and watched me getting beaten half to death, even my own friend. He's always said there were too many enemies for him to help me, but I swear that if it had been the other way round I'd have rushed to protect him.

In the middle of the blows, I could tell one of my attackers was particularly evil. He hit me ten times harder than anyone else with what felt like a blunt object. If you've never been hit around the head I can tell you that when it happens you start to see flashes of white or yellow. Like your brain is being shaken. The only other way to describe the feeling is imagine whacking the back of your TV and for a split second the picture turns fuzzy then back to normal. I don't know how long the attack lasted but it felt like forever.

The DJ who'd played a set in the club was the only one who had the balls to pull some of my attackers from me. As they backed-off, out of the corner of my eye I noticed a beer bottle, and with around ten years of fights and violence on the streets my instincts came into play. I believed in my now disoriented state that I was indeed fighting for my life, and in a flash I grabbed the bottle then smashed it to defend myself. The CCTV showed my attackers backing off as I lunged at them with it. The bottle shone under the streetlights as I swung it in the direction of these hyenas, it was time to separate the men from the boys. All of them backed off as I stumbled towards them waving the bottle menacingly.

Whilst all of this was going on I can put my hands up and honestly say I didn't know what I was doing. After being hit with force over the head and with the number of times I was assaulted you could say I was concussed. This was confirmed by the CCTV footage; you can clearly see my head making these weird circular movements as I stumbled toward the watching crowd. What happened next was the act of an injured, scared and desperate man. I walked into the crowd and without further thought stabbed the bottle into the side of an onlooker's head, then turned to his friend and struck the bottle into his neck.

All I can remember from that point is sitting in the back of a police van in handcuffs. It wasn't until I viewed the footage that I recognised the extreme violence I'd committed. It turned-out the men I stabbed were innocent bystanders just watching the drama unfold and they happened to be in the wrong place at the wrong time. It's crazy how things turn out, whilst walking into that club for a party I didn't have the slightest clue that I'd stab someone and that the DJ would save my life! In my crazed mind I thought the two men I stabbed were going to attack me. So, before anybody says it wasn't self-defence, it was seconds after the last attacker backed off. It all happened so quickly that the police who watched me get savagely beaten didn't even realise I'd harmed anyone. In their statements they wrote only that they saw Justin Rollins punch two people. I never meant to hurt those innocent men and felt sorry for them but around the time it happened I was on another planet.

My head was absolutely battered; there were scratches, wounds and lumps as big as tennis balls as well as purple bruises and trainer marks across my face and body. I felt like I'd done ten rounds with Mike Tyson with my hands tied behind my back! I was driven the short distance to Sutton Police Station and taken into the custody suite. They made me stand in front of the sergeant, two police officers had to hold me straight as I was wobbling all over the show. I didn't have the slightest clue why I was there. I didn't know where I was. I did know I'd been battered though and asked them to take me to hospital.

I saw I was surrounded by policemen and in my concussed state they were the enemy. 'Why am I here, take me to hospital,' I screamed. Yes, I have a history of violence but never towards the police, but I believe I started acting in an extremely aggressive manner. If you research concussion it isn't hard to find examples of normal people acting in a violent manner after a head injury. With my history and my injuries I think my aggressive demeanour was enhanced ten-fold. I refused to give them my name and was uncontrollable for nearly an hour.

I was taken to a holding cell, stripped of my clothes and footwear to be sent to forensics and given a white jumper, white bottoms and plimsolls. I lay on a pissy mattress and later on I was discovered barely conscious covered in my own vomit. Two police officers then whisked me off to St Helier Hospital to be examined by a 'wonderful' NHS doctor. What a great idea to let me be seen by a the same person who'd only an hour before stitched the wounds I'd inflicted on two other men.

When I did finally start to get better around a fortnight later all of this haunted me for weeks on end. The doctor had screamed, 'There's nothing wrong with you, pathetic, pathetic.' He then asked the officers if I was to be released, near enough begging them to keep me locked-up. He told them that the wounds I'd inflicted on the other guys were 'of military precision.' And with that I was slung back in the meat wagon with two rookie cops and taken back to the police station. It was a bumpy ride and I didn't bother to get-up from the floor after I came flying off the cold metal seat. I just lay there helpless.

All of a sudden, the meat wagon came to a halt, the doors were ripped open, and two officers stood over me. We weren't at the police station but in a car park four blocks away. The officers began to pinch my face and dig their thumbs into pressure points under my jaw and behind my ear, so they said to see if I was alive. I never even felt the pain they were trying to dish out, my body was so numb from the brutal beating I'd received earlier.

'YOU ALIVE BOY, YOU ALIVE?' they screamed, then started to slap me around the face. I still have nightmares and flashbacks of those moments, as in my confused state I believed that the officers were going to kill me. They said they were checking to see if I was conscious and well enough to be brought into custody, most probably to save their own skins if I happened to die in their hands. After a few slurred words to them they hopped back in the wagon and drove me to the station.

At crack of dawn I was led into the custody area. This was it. This was my time to tell the custody officer that I was about to be killed by the arresting officers. This was my only chance for survival. I started to shout, 'Help fucking help, they're going to kill me, they fucking tried to do me in down the road, help, help.' The custody officers just laughed. I was dragged by the handcuffs and my wrists bled as my body scraped along the floor. I screamed the house down, 'Help their gonna kill me, help!' I was bounced off every wall then bundled face first into a cell where I landed on my front. They unlocked the cuffs and more officers pinned me down as they counted down from five to one as each got up and ran from the cell. The cold metal door slammed hard behind them and with that and in my heavily concussed mind I ripped-off a piece from the shitty, white police issue jumper and made it into a noose. I wrapped it as hard as I could around my neck and tied it into a knot. This next part is so dark for me that it gives me flashbacks still. It deeply traumatised my already damaged mind.

This was not a cry for help like my old party tricks, I was lucky to be alive. I choked so bad that I turned blue, and I had red dots all around my face from lack of air. The cell door flew open as an army of officers jumped on me, slamming me to the ground. Not being able to breathe, my eyes felt like they were about to pop. My arms were pulled behind my back in a restraining position; one evil officer pulled them so far up my back they stuck there. Another cut through the noose with a pair of scissors. FUCK. FINALLY I COULD BREATHE. Then an officer cut off my jumper, tracksuit bottoms and boxer shorts as I was held down. They grabbed my clothes, my blanket and mattress and ran from the cell.

I lay on my front, praying for air as I started hyperventilating. The deep breathing was so loud it hurt my ears, I was terrified, I felt like I'd been sexually assaulted. I lay on that cold floor naked for probably an hour as I did not have an ounce of strength to pull my arms back down from the restraining position. This is in the top three of the worst experiences I've ever been through in my extremely disturbed and fucked-up young life. I was battered, heavily bruised, naked, gasping for breath and lying there helpless. I still didn't have a clue why I was being held as I thought it was only me who'd been attacked. 'Why the fuck am I being treated like this?' I thought to myself.

Then out of nowhere I seemed to gather some immense fighting spirit. 'NO FUCKING WAY AM I GOING TO BE TREATED LIKE THIS!' I knew those evil pigs were on the other side of the door watching me, they were happy that I'd given in, that I was a broken man. 'FUCK THAT! NO WAY!' With all my strength I pulled my arms from behind my back and slowly got to my feet. I stood there naked with the officer in the custody area watching my movements on CCTV. I was like a hamster in a lab. With all my mental energy I started to kick the door so hard it bruised my feet. This was to show them I wasn't down anymore, I may have been absolutely battered but I was still standing. They hadn't broken me; I was still alive and kicking!

When challenged about injuring two men with a broken bottle, I was too mentally and physically drained to answer their accusations. I gave a no comment interview. I'm sure they could see that I was an utter mess. I learned I'd been arrested on two charges of 'GBH with intent.' Each carried a maximum sentence of life in prison, so I'd be banged up for a seriously long time if convicted. If I'd been treated like an innocent man defending himself, I might just have got away with it. But with my record I was treated like a brutal, vicious thug who'd hurt two innocent victims. The detectives never acknowledged that I'd been highly provoked and was in no state to figure out who was friend or foe. Even if they knew it was a terrible mistake, a case of an unwell man fighting for survival, they never said so. They told me they had to 'follow the law,' but at least would be granting me bail pending further enquires. As I left the police station one officer shouted, 'You get yourself to hospital boy.' And with that I left there utterly broken.

CHAPTER 15

Searching for Answers

How the hell do you go out for a party with your mate and end up on bail for GBH? Especially if you've taken a beating and look like you've been run over by a bus. Fuck me, talking of transport, when I left the police station I started looking for my car. After 20 minutes I had a memory of using my keys to defend myself and must have dropped them, only then for one of my attackers to see them, pick them up and nick my car. Fuck, fuck, fuck! Talk about kicking a man when he's down. I found myself back in Sutton Police Station reporting that my car had been stolen. Feeling unfortunate is an understatement, I was well and truly shafted.

I never went back to the hospital. No, I made my way to mother's house. She freaked-out on seeing the state I was in, but I just went up to my old room and collapsed on the bed. I lay there for three days only getting-up for the toilet or a quick bite to eat. My life was once again in free fall, a complete disaster. I didn't have a clue how to dig myself out of the grave I'd created. I was facing a lengthy sentence if convicted, but in my mind it was clearly self-defence. I found I no longer had an ounce of strength to make sense of all that had happened and I slipped into a dark depression, acting oddly and contemplating suicide daily.

After a week I headed home to my maisonette and locked myself away from the world. I believe I started to have a nervous breakdown and could no longer cope with the pressure. I lay in bed most days and it got to the point where I couldn't leave the house at all. I'd cry my eyes out over the slightest thing, such as not having food in the fridge. I wanted to die so badly, I just wanted this crazy life to go away, to end. Yes, I'd got really drunk in the club and was carrying a bad energy to attract trouble, but surely I didn't deserve to be treated worse than a dog by my attackers, the hospital doctor and the police. 'Those bastards won,' I thought, 'and I no longer have any fight left in my soul.' Though I wished my life would just end, I didn't even have the strength to kill myself! I remember being scared and nervous if I heard a noise or bang at my front door. I'd get-up to see what it was armed with a hammer, believing it was my attackers coming to finish me off. It was usually only the postman or leaflet distributors.

One morning I picked-up the local paper and on the front page there was a photo of the night club where the madness had happened and the headline 'Club LOVE-2-LOVE, But Where's the Love.' I read of a mass brawl and how two men had been stabbed. 'What the fuck,' I thought. 'They never get it right, mass fucking brawl? Okay if you can call one man being savagely beaten by a crowd a "mass brawl."'

In my depressed, frustrated state I started to tear the newspaper to bits, screaming obscenities at the top of my voice. Because of the music at that club it said it would attract the wrong crowd. In other words if a club is to play rap and RnB music it will attract groups of men looking for trouble. Yes, rap music and music in general has an effect on one's mind, and Gangsta rap especially with its violent lyrics but this club never played that. What it did do though is play the type of rap and RnB songs that glamorise 'money, fast cars, fast girls and bling.' You only have to turn on your music channel to hear this type of music with its hard aggressive beats. With a bunch of young men trying to show the girls their muscles and the amount of money they've got by popping bottles of champagne there is going to be rivalry and chancers looking to make some sort of name for themselves.

Sutton being on the borders of South West London you'd have many gangs coming there from the inner-city. Around two weeks after I stabbed the two men, a major incident occurred. Two rival South London gangs had an altercation outside LOVE-2-LOVE, only for one of them to run-off to collect his shooter, a sawn-off shot gun. He then plodded across the road from the club and thinking he saw his rivals leaving fired two rounds into the crowd. It was a miracle no-one was hit or killed. After the stabbings and the gun being fired the club shut down permanently. It's now a distant memory.

Around two weeks later my stolen car was involved in a high-speed police chase, only for the driver to abandon the vehicle and to try to make his getaway on foot. He was arrested but I never heard the outcome. I wouldn't press charges but the police still had their own power to convict him as they never needed my consent. I did think of finding-out his court date so I could watch him from the public gallery and learn of his identity and address to seek some sort of sick revenge, but I just left it. What was the point? I attack him, he comes after me, and it goes on and on and on.

The police had also arrested five of my attackers and contacted me to see if I'd press charges against them. I was not going to give those bastard police what they wanted and even though I wished to watch my attackers suffer I never said a word. I'm sure the police still had grounds to charge them with violent disorder and to this day I haven't a clue who they were or what the outcome was. When I finally got my car back it was empty of my designer sunglasses, CDs and iPod.

With no car to drive I'd found going out even harder as at that time I never had the confidence to walk around alone. Those bastards had really broken me, I cried and cried. 'WHY THE FUCK AM I CRYING, WHY, WHY, WHY?' I just couldn't understand why I was so messed-up over the beating. 'WHAT'S WRONG WITH ME, FUCK, FUCK, WHY CAN'T I HANDLE THIS? I'M USED TO TAKING BEATINGS, I'M USED TO VIOLENCE, I CAN NORMALLY HANDLE A HIDING!' Shock swept through my body as for the first time in my destructive, messed-up life I realised VIOLENCE ISN'T NORMAL, NO-ONE SHOULD BE USED TO BEING BEATEN!

Up until that point of my life stabbing or being stabbed *was* normal, being kicked or kicking someone *was* normal, but in fact in a civilised world this definitely *isn't* normal. Though I hated my attackers at the time of the event, they actually knocked some sense into me. If it wasn't for that I'd probably still be involved in some sort of violence and would not be the man that sits here today writing this for you. It opened-up a part of my brain that led me onto 'light at the end of the tunnel.' It was like planting a seed and watching it grow. Though I was still in a dark frame of mind and never realised that seed would grow and blossom I'd begun to lead a more normal life, turning things around so much that I'd no longer be respected or feared around my town for being a lunatic. I'd be respected for telling it how it really is through my writing! In the meantime, I was still serving a 'nervous breakdown.' It led to depression and flashbacks of those crazy times on the streets spraying my graffiti tag.

I hadn't done graffiti for years but found this to be my new therapy, to help me overcome my stress and pain. Walking those railways late at night seemed to temporally heal my wounds. But then it started to make me feel even more fucked-up. After talking with my mum some nights she convinced me it was time to go to see somebody about my problems. My first thoughts were negative, like 'Fuck that I ain't seeing anyone ... what can those mugs do for me?' Two weeks later I found myself in a drug awareness centre where they offered free counselling. The thing is I never had an issue with drugs, but I'd been told that they offered free top quality one-to-one therapy. Not being one to lie, I sat there and told them it straight, 'Look I'm fucked-up, I don't really have a drug problem, but I have a drink problem and many other issues.' After telling them a few brutal stories they sat there in shock!

It was against their policy to offer anyone not involved with drugs any sort of help. But with them seeing I was so desperately in need of it those wonderful people bent the rules. As in my teenage years I'd had a few issues with drugs, they led me to believe that my current state of mind and my current drink problem maybe stemmed from drugs initially. Two ladies from the organization put these words into my mouth while I just sat back and nodded approvingly.

I can see the two women had hearts of gold and they showed that by reaching-out to help me and giving me a push in the right direction. I don't think they will ever know or feel what they did for me in that moment; their actions played such a great role in my rehabilitation. I had to sit two further assessments and was then put on a waiting list until the right therapist was found, but my foot was in the door. A step in the right direction.

In the meantime, I remained on bail on the GBH charges and after six weeks I was called to Sutton Police Station. I made hopeless prayers that I'd be let off with no further action. But I was fingerprinted, photographed and then charged with two counts of 'GBH section 18 with intent.' I shouldn't have been given bail but because of the circumstances and the fact I'd already returned to them on bail I was granted it.

My solicitor told me, 'Yes, it looks like self-defence' but at the same time I'd cut two innocent bystanders so there was a problem. His words left my mind all over the place as to what would be the outcome at court. If I was to plead not guilty the jury might find me guilty as they would feel sorry for the victims. Surely though they would see I was actually the victim for once in my life. The solicitor wouldn't comment further. In the meantime he swore to find me the 'very best barrister' he could to represent me at Croydon Crown Court.

My time was now spent biting my fingernails, worrying about my upcoming court case as I walked the streets with my dog. Both our heads were down as the depression would not leave me. I'd all but forgotten my assessment at the drug awareness centre until I received a voice message telling me a therapist had been found and that I could start my sessions in just a few days' time. This was it, the time had come to relive my past in that small but comforting therapy room searching for answers, There would be tears and there would be laughter. But most of all there would be a force for change.

CHAPTER 16

It's Good to Talk

A part from a few sessions with Rachel the psychologist at Aylesbury Prison I'd never sat with a professional therapist, opened-up about my old war wounds and talked of my past. From a young age, my way of dealing with issues was to express them through self-destruction, anger, drinking, vandalism and in other chaotic ways. Like many young adults my brain was still developing so it was difficult to understand emotions and feelings, especially when they were all over the show like mine. If you're not taught to express your feelings as a child, not listened to and have emotionally absent parents you grow-up confused and with problems. I remember the first time I sat in front of the therapist, I looked her over with what I called 'hyper-scanning,' checking-out her body language to see if she could be trusted.

I reckon she got around ten words out of me the first hourly session. I left in the usual angry mood, but something must have felt good about it as I returned the following week. Could I trust this lady? Would she go to the police or courts and tell them I was a nutter? Looking back, you could say I'd zero trust for 99.9 per cent of the people I came across, but something about the therapist was different and I felt at ease. As we entered the fourth week of sessions, I started to open-up properly and talk of my family and early childhood. I described my emotionally absent mother always being at work, and then I told her about the time I was abused at the childminder's as a small boy. That the childminder's teenage son used to strangle me with fishing wire when I was only five years old. Though it was two decades ago I remembered those incidents clearly. The childminder would go out and leave the kids in her care a lot; we then had to fend for ourselves against her son. After telling the therapist this story she sat there for a while with a caring look on her face. Then told me that the events that I'd experienced were 'child abuse.' I tried to fob her off saying it was nothing as for all those years I just thought it was normal.

Normal to be strangled? WHAT THE FUCK! We pinpointed the change in my character after these incidents, from my anxiety to starting stealing, to me going into school and striking another child with a pair of scissors. I don't know what the childminder told my mother, but I was sent back to her full of anxiety. Why wasn't my mother protecting me? But as a five-year-old I didn't have the capacity to blame my Mum, so I blamed myself. A child needs protecting, but I was not protected for whatever reason. So I grew inwards, I developed a core belief that I was not good enough. That I must be a bad kid. This was the first time I'd dug up my past and started to examine it with a professional. After the sessions I felt totally drained. Once I headed back to my mother's house the questions carried on in my head. I became angry with her for leaving me in the care of that childminder and we had many arguments.

I poured my life out in those sessions and began slowly to like myself even if only slightly, I started to look at the good parts of my life. Such as my daughter, my family, my kindness to others and what I hoped was a talent for writing. I told the therapist that it was my dream to write of my experiences and have my own book on the shelf. I believed that dreams were in fact just dreams and never actually came true. But I started to talk about my future, instead of sitting there dredging-up my miserable past.

I also told the therapist of my love for weight training as I believed that having a healthy body meant having a healthy mind. I remember clearly one day walking into a local gym looking anxious and asking the man on reception about joining. He told me to go into the weights room and look around and that is what I did. I remember seeing these tall body-building geezers built like brick shithouses, dripping with sweat and screaming and shouting as they threw their weights around. I thought, 'Fuck me, it's rough in here.' But rough I was also, and I joined the same day. I didn't then know that this mean machine of a place would become a big part of my life and help with my rehabilitation. It was called Pinks Gym, owned by Peter Pink, a bodybuilding place of the old school type that was also a community hub. That sort of gym is rare nowadays, with 24-hour premises popping up everywhere for people on the go and they've lost the community feel of a gym like Pinks.

When I explained to the therapist I'd joined and was going four-to-five times every week she was most impressed. You have to remember my social skills were near zero as I was used to mixing with street people, convicts, nutters and winos. I'd never been in an environment with ordinary guys that worked and had decent lives and their own families. It was a massive step for me to even enter the place. At first, I didn't speak to anyone as I was always suspicious of other people, and just got on with my training, but as the weeks went by I got talking to them. I was still in my early-twenties and wanted to get 'hench' meaning big and muscly. I didn't realise that by doing so it was me still trying to protect myself. I thought the bigger and meaner I looked the less chance of being attacked. It worked, I did look menacing and of course I could be extremely violent. But in reality, if someone really wants to hurt you they won't care about your size. There was a good side to the intense training and that was the discipline and the exercise which was a brilliant stress reliever if only for a short while. I started to fit in.

I was changing fast and for the better. I never saw Gabriella as a problem or some sort of unwanted responsibility anymore, I saw her as my future and though I might go to prison I'd be there for her on my release. It was like something had clicked in my brain, almost overnight, and I bonded with my child and she became the most precious thing to ever touch my life. Unconditional love, wow that feeling was crazy. I began to realise how delicate a child's mind is, and that Gabriella needed me. I was still young and unwise, I thought I was healed. But I was at least coping better and moving forward step-by-step in a more positive way.

I was invited out for the birthday celebrations of one of the gym guys and was happy about this, it felt great that I was accepted. Before that I'd never really been to nice clubs or social events. I'd missed the years of going out to parties and clubs as I was in prison. So, this was a big thing for me. Around ten of us went to a club in London and had a wicked time. I looked around at the energy from my new friends and it was all laughs and smiles. I was used to my old friends drinking and fighting, we were all criminals, thugs, and a lot of them were wrong-uns. But my new friends were bouncers, train drivers, delivery men and others held down nine-to-five jobs. They never knew of my past or my reputation as a thug and nutter. The older guys gave me advice on bringing up a child, and they all accepted me for who I was, which made me feel good and like myself if only just a bit. And due to the exercise and training my mind and body were healthier. I'd get looks from the ladies and this would make me feel great. For years I'd looked in the mirror and seen an 'ugly Paki' staring back. Now with a new circle of friends and looking in great shape I actually started to respect myself and attempted to love myself. Obviously not to the degree of somebody that carries a mirror in their pocket but in the sense that I started to like the person I was becoming: stronger, more positive and most of all a great father to my daughter.

I'd lost my driving licence a long time back for being reckless so this made it difficult to get out and about with Gabriella. But I wasn't going to be a man that made excuses, it was my own fault and I had to accept responsibility. So, I forgot about a car and with a one-day travel card me and my daughter were off. From taking her to the London Aquarium, to London Zoo, to just sitting down with her making nice things, baking cakes and painting, I loved every minute of it, seeing her grow and seeing her cry for her Daddy just melted my heart. My older friends at the gym told me to enjoy it while she was still young and that is what I did — and ever since.

The therapist was so impressed with my change over the eight months that she wrote me a good report for court that gave me a slim hope that I wouldn't go to prison. Had I earned this possibility through my change of character? I believe I had. Even if I did go to prison, I'd deal with it in a positive way as I'd come too far to back down now. Fingers crossed even though sentencing was ... on Friday thirteenth.

I finally got to meet my barrister who was highly rated by his colleagues. He told me that I should plead guilty at court but on the basis of 'a high level of provocation' and ask the judge to view the CCTV footage of the brutal beating I took. In the meantime he would do a plea bargain with the prosecutor on the terms that if they lowered the charges from GBH with intent to straight GBH I'd be willing to plead guilty, making it easier on the victims as they would not have to give evidence. One of them wrote in his statement that he saw me being attacked by around 40 men and the other that I was being attacked by 25 (my guess is it was just 14). So these statements only helped my cause.

I remember watching my barrister joking with the prosecutor and realised they were buddies. I began to think that if I'd used a barrister from the other side of London, who wasn't used to working in that court, he would probably not have known the prosecutor, so when asking for a plea bargain it would be like asking a stranger for a favour, that if you use a barrister that is known and respected in the court you are summoned to you are more likely to get a better result. And if your barrister genuinely likes you and believes you shouldn't go to prison then he will tell his mate this, and they'll help you out. That's why I think he got the charge reduced. Once the judge knew of the beating that I'd taken and with my reacting violently with a bottle for just seconds after I was attacked my barrister reckoned I'd get a two year prison sentence. I'd serve just a year if I behaved in jail, with a further three months taken off on tag in the community.

CHAPTER 17

A Locked Mind

It was the first time I'd sat in a court awaiting a prison sentence when not feeling the slightest anxiety. I'd prepared myself for months and believed I'd changed into a positive person. Yes, I'd hurt two innocent men, and, yes, I never had the slightest clue what was going on when I struck-out with a broken bottle, but it was time to man up, to face the consequences.

An ordinary man who had never been involved in violence might have walked away relatively lightly. But due to my violent past I wasn't going to be treated like your average Joe. I could cry about it, self-harm, get angry, go absolutely mental, but what good would that have done. I now had a daughter who needed me in her life, yeah Daddy was going away for a while but he'd be back. Back stronger than ever.

I handed my barrister the report from my therapist. After reading it he told me that it was so supportive of my change of character that he'd do all he could to get me a community sentence. He also pointed out that I'd sought therapy before I'd even been charged with the offences, therefore this wasn't some cunning ploy. Yes, I genuinely went to the therapist because I wanted to change.

Friday the thirteenth was meant to be a day when things went wrong. When I told people I was to be sentenced on the thirteenth they each had some sort of superstition that things would not go my way and I'd end up with five years in jail! But I never took on their negative vibes and hoped for maybe a two-year sentence. The judge went out to watch the CCTV of my beating, that is all of it that my clever barrister showed her, well he wasn't about to highlight me stabbing two people five minutes before the judge was about to sentence me. He then went through the therapist's report as I waited patiently behind a glass screen with a guard either side. The female guard whispered, 'Surely you can't go to prison for this, you were the victim.' I hoped her words were true.

The judge returned and I was told to rise. 'Justin Rollins, this is a very unusual case. In my judgment you were acting in self-defence, but at the same time you hurt two innocent young men. If it wasn't for your history of violence you may very well have walked free. But I've no option but to punish you. I've taken into consideration your enormous change of character over the last eight-to-nine months and that you haven't been convicted of a violent offence for some years, so I will sentence you to one year in prison...'

I sat there thinking, 'I knew it. I knew I'd get a prison term' until I heard the judge continue, '... suspended for two years, and a two-year probation order, and you must attend a ten-week Anger Replacement Therapy course. She then added that I must carry out 200 hours community service and pay each victim compensation of £500. 'Mr Rollins if you break any of these terms you'll be brought back before me faster than you know it.' With that I was released feeling dizzy and numb. I was greeted and cheered by my friends as I left court. What the hell had just happened? I was in total shock that I'd just walked away from an immediate prison sentence.

I wasn't jumping around for joy as I was gobsmacked, more mentally drained than anything. I thanked my barrister and he told me that if it wasn't for the therapist's contribution I'd have surely been sitting in the cells below waiting for a van to Wandsworth. The best thing though is that I was actually getting some recognition for my change of character. For once the system was not against me and I was not against it.

I wondered what the two victims thought of the outcome. Did they want me to rot in jail? Did they know that I'd been in such a daze at the time of assaulting them that I didn't understand what I was doing to them? I may never know. I'd always felt bad for them but it was time to move on. I never wanted to be a victim again and I certainly never wanted to create any more victims. I'd had enough of being looked down on by old associates who'd moved on in their lives. Enough of being feared for violence. Enough of being a negative, messed-up young man. I wanted to turn it all around and come back stronger than ever and that's what I was determined to do.

When I was a 15-year-old street kid out-and-about stealing food, spray paint and money with my gang I'd wander off and nick books from WHSmith, then late at night whether sleeping in a bus garage or train depot I'd sit and read. The stories took me far away from my reality of pain and desperation. As the years went by and I experienced more and more chaotic and disturbing things I knew that I had my own story to tell. It is quite funny as in the middle of a crazy moment I'd think, 'This will be great in my book.' I'd tell my friends that I was going to write a book, but I doubt many of them believed me as they were more into rapping. Back then I'd rap too, but I just saw it as a fashionable thing to do.

As you know I can be extreme with my thinking and even though many friends created good rap music I never believed they'd make it, as thousands of kids were doing the same thing and sounding the same, with similar lyrics and topics. What else would we rap about, working-class and street issues were the theme. But because I wrote poetry which I'd then rap I realised how I pulled the listener in at the start, the middle was the main point of the tale and the end used to have to leave the listener thinking or shocked. So as my friends all rapped the same sort of way, I began to look at it as I might a chapter, use the same thinking. I didn't want to be like everyone else in my community and I certainly didn't want to be like the old villains who wrote books about how tough they were. But back then I was a talker, I never actually thought I'd sit down and do it, write an autobiography.

After I never received a prison sentence for the attacks, I bought myself a laptop and started to write of my experiences. I sent the first three chapters to my friend Joe's dad, Noel 'Razor' Smith who is a bestselling author and respected writer and he said he loved what he read. It added to my confidence when he told me, 'Don't change anything, just keep writing, so far it's great.' I was excited; I was actually writing the book I'd always dreamed of. I was going to be a success. After writing about my life from my birth to age 18 I ended it there. I named my book *The Lost Boyz: A Dark Side of Graffiti.* 'This is it, I've made it,' I thought to myself.

But my naïve mind never knew how hard it was going to be to get published. I spent so much in printing and posting costs to only get replies of, 'Sorry this isn't for us,' or 'We're currently not taking on any more works, all the best.' These were setbacks and at times the responses made me question whether my work was anywhere near good enough. But I knew it was. I was sure that if I kept pushing for a publishing deal I'd get it, I'd finally bring things full circle, come back to my manor and be respected for turning my life around. People could then read about this character Sevens that hung on their local streets causing trouble and drama for years, but this time they could read about the real reasons behind my actions, that there was a method behind my madness.

Then came success! After two years of contacting publishers, being led down false avenues, being sucked in by con men making you think that they want your work then only to ask for large sums of money, after all that stress and fight I finally got my break. A criminal justice publisher called Waterside Press showed interest in my work and believed in it, yes it was an autobiography but at the same time could be read and studied in sociology and criminology circles. In my mind I was still thinking, 'It could be another scam.' After weeks of waiting I got the phone call that I'd hoped for, they wanted to publish *The Lost Boyz*. I gritted my teeth and literally jumped with joy. I'd fucking made it, my shit past wasn't for nothing; I felt shivers all over my body.

Those times I was treated like a dog by prison officers, the time I lost my best mate, the time I was brutally beaten, every fucking bad, sad or mad thing that had happened to me wasn't going to be for nothing after all. It was all worth it. I was coming back from the dead. So proud I was, so positive I felt at that point. In a naïve way I believed that I was healed, like having a book published would suddenly rescue me from my mental health issues just like that. I couldn't have been so wrong. Becoming published gave me a focus, but I'd no-one pointing me in the right direction concerning what to do next. Looking back, when I first started writing that earlier book it was about bragging, 'Look at me this gang leader, this hard man, this gangster.' It's sad isn't it, all for ego and greed? But when I put pen to paper it is like my pen wouldn't let me write lies. The gangster life wasn't fun, I didn't win every fight and at times I sat there and cried. So, the writing never came out as this hard tough man, it was brutally honest and told it like it really was, like this one does. The book would take me on a new journey, meeting different people and realising the world wasn't full of killers and evil sos and sos that I'd spent so much time with.

Then 25 years old, I started to learn about who I was, my background, upbringing and so on. When my book was published, that was a lot of pressure for me with everything that I'd seen. Coming out of a gang life and prison there was a lot of hatred towards me. I made a documentary that got over 30,000 views on YouTube, and I came across as if I was arrogant and self-satisfied about some of the violence I was talking about. It's strange looking at that video now, I look so damaged in my eyes. I was indeed a very impaired young man. I was huge with muscle and looked intimidating, whilst most of the people I grew up with enjoyed my old war stories. But some of the comments I got were nasty. This fuelled the paranoia I was trying to convince myself I never had.

After getting into the local press a few times, papers like the *London Evening Standard* picked it up. At one stage I was a regular on LBC with Nick Ferrari, Iane Dale and other presenters. I never knew at the time that I was well-spoken and articulate when talking on crime and gangs, I was just being me. Many times I had offers to do talks at universities and to carry-out youth work, but in the beginning I just wasn't ready for it. I'd be up at night freaking-out about being in a new environment. The morning would come and all of a sudden I'd be ill. I'd cancel so many work opportunities due to panic attacks. Then I'd sit there all day feeling guilty for not showing-up and being conscious of what they must have felt about me. I wasn't well, but I didn't know how unwell. All I really knew is that I found everyday life extremely stressful. I was in a healing process but it would take a very long time before I felt at a mental level where I could interact normally with people.

I stuck to promoting my efforts on social media and pushing my book to news outlets, which was pretty successful. With no agent and just hard work I found myself being filmed for ITV documentaries like 'Exposure: A Life on The Run' with Mark Williams-Thomas and though they didn't air me in the final version they invited me onto 'This Morning' to talk about being on the run and I was interviewed by Eamonn Holmes and Ruth Langford. Later that day my Facebook page went crazy all about how I was on live TV, and I realised my book was a massive thing in my community. The love was outweighing the hate, in some people's eyes I was a hero. I know it sounds strange and I sometimes found it cringing and hard to take. But coming from where I did and the class that I associated myself with it was huge. Writing a book and being published just wasn't done in our community. I ran with some of the lowest of the low, I'd seen extreme violence and witnessed death: friends murdered or who had been murderers. I'd spent time with the country's most barbaric killers. To even be alive was a miracle, so to write a book and to get it published was so big for everyone where I came from.

I was filmed for a Channel 5 documentary 'Dangerous Dog Owners and Proud' and helped them meet people for the programme. After speaking about pitbulls they never used my part, but my phone number was out there and I became a go between for media outlets and the streets. BBC news came to film me about prison violence and that got a lot of attention. But Wayne Lister was still with me. I'd walk down the street and see someone staring at me, the hairs on my back would go up and I'd stare back with menace. I was afraid it was an old gang member or someone from prison that was after me. From years of street and prison life I could give off a look and vibe that would scare many people, I never felt nice doing it and the person I was watching didn't feel nice either. But that was my protection and the way I reacted to previous trauma. I was living in fight or flight mode and most of the time ready to turn. I scanned virtually everything, my hypervigilance was extreme. I'd spot people before they spotted me. I could read body language a mile off. How embarrassing when the person approached nervously and said he loved my book! I felt like an idiot. The paranoia got me in trouble so many times, even at that stage I still slept with an axe next to my bed in case old foes kicked my front door off.

With local fame came attention from women, those that spotted me in newspapers to those who'd see me on TV, they contacted me through Facebook. I was never confident with such things, how could I be when I was so damaged. I didn't trust a soul, it's embarrassing to say so but if a woman looked at me when I was in the street I thought it was because they were sticking their nose up at me, or they were fearful. I never once thought it was that they may have liked the look of me.

When I didn't have my daughter with me, I'd often be alone in my flat; I never realised at the time what prison had done to me. Being institutionalised made me go home for the evening like I was being locked-up for the night. If I was away from home and it was getting towards seven in the evening, I'd find myself heading there as quickly as possible because I was used to being banged-up at that time in prison. I even had a security gate fitted at my house so I felt secure and no other prisoners could get in to hurt me. In reality prison was years in my past but my mind was locked. I saw neighbours as prisoners, and anyone with authority was a prison officer. I was still doing time in my mind, and I wondered if it was a life sentence. All the while this was running through my mind I was still doing book signings and promoting myself in any newspaper that would listen. But sometimes the anxiety became too much to even meet with a reporter, so I'd do a phone or email interview. This meant that I needed some photos taken to send to them along with my story. I was given the phone number of a friend of a friend that I'd never met before called Daisy.

We arranged to meet back in Sutton, and I waited patiently by the station for her. What met me was the most beautiful person I'd ever seen. I don't care what people say, it was love at first sight. She was only 18 and I was 25 which was a big gap in my eyes but from that moment I was hooked. She introduced herself with a big smile and perfect teeth.

After we finished taking photos by a level crossing she said the pictures would be ready in a week. Sitting home alone I couldn't stop thinking about how beautiful she was, but that after a few days I'd get her out of my system as 'I don't fall in love' or so I thought. 'Gang members and leaders don't fall in love, that stuff is for pussies ... Plus I never let women get too close.'

The week passed and I went to collect a memory stick. Seeing Daisy again that earlier feeling came over me. I said I should take her out sometime and she agreed. But I never heard from her and was convinced she wasn't really interested. I was having a battle between falling in love and being me! Eventually I built up the courage and texted her, still worried about her being 18 and me 25, but I made contact anyway. She said she'd love to meet and we went on our first date. That was it, I needed her, she was the purest person I'd met in my brutal life. I fell in love with Daisy and she did with me.

My life before Daisy was full of hate and people who bad mouthed and abused others. Daisy never said a bad word about anyone. Her whole vibe was love, I looked at her and she floated. She was the opposite of me, I never did float, I stomped the ground and people knew I was coming. She was oblivious to negative thoughts, smart, aware, with so much love and kindness she only saw the positive side. She grew up with her mum and dad, but as a child spent a lot of time with her grandparents who she adored. They were from a different generation. They grew old together and were the sort that sat on the beach holding hands, eating ice cream, growing old and grey. With today's generation I can see that sort dying out. With social media and dating sites and apps dating has become like a playground and there is so much temptation out there.

Many of my close friends are single and have a negative view of women even today. I always say, 'But what about me and Daisy?' They say, 'Yeah but

Daisy's different.' I ask them why. I believe you attract what you think about, so if you're negative about something that's what you'll see. I see me and Daisy like her Nan and Grandad, not like my great grandparents, they split up, so did my grandparents, then my parents and even Sarah and I did. Daisy lay in my arms, she brought peace to me.

I'd sworn to myself that I'd never bring a woman around my daughter, because if you remember, to me everything was a threat. When Gabriella first met Daisy she had just turned four, she hugged me while looking at her and said, 'My Daddy.' Daisy was perfect with her and they soon bonded. Daisy's younger energy was high, she was confident, always dancing and singing. She brought stability into our lives. I'd never realised just how feral I'd become: one plate, knife and fork plus a child's set. When Daisy stayed over I had to go out and buy extra crockery and cutlery.

My anxiety had an effect on Gabriella's early life, I'd try my best to take her out and do normal things, but my paranoia limited it. When I first took her to a play centre, I'd just freeze. I was convinced other parents looked at me like I was a freak with my scars and tattoos. Gabriella stayed close to my side and in those early days she was very shy. But I was trying, I'd take her to a Little Theatre show some Sundays. One day when I was there it was sing-a-long time, but there was another dad there that looked a bit streetwise in my eyes. My anxiety and ego made me freeze. All the other dads were waving their arms but me, and Gabriella sat frozen. I told myself, 'Fuck it, just go for it,' and there I was with the other dads waving my arms and singing. I nearly passed out I was so on edge.

Daisy is stunning, when we would be out going about our business other men used to and still do stare at her. I loved her back then and still do now, I trust her, and she trusts me. But when men stared at her and I looked towards them all I saw was eyes like those of Wayne Lister coming back onto the prison unit and staring at me with hatred. I'd stare back with that menacing Aylesbury look. Maybe if I couldn't break down how I felt, it would look like I was jealous or controlling, but that was far from the case. I had trust issues with past women, but not with Daisy.

I didn't cause arguments or accuse Daisy of stuff. She was different, she was the ying to my yang, and brought a sense of calmness to me. Though I was changing it was a slow process. I was still freaked out from Aylesbury issues,

I'd wake up in the middle of the night screaming for help, rolling around the bed, even shouting out for my Mum, but Daisy would be there to reassure me that nobody was coming to get me.

I realised that seeing the therapist for those sessions I described earlier was not going to heal me just like that. I'd seen, received and done a lot of damage and I still hated myself. It was time to find a new therapist.

CHAPTER 18

Old Wounds to Heal

My new therapist was older and more experienced. It was difficult to express the fear I had of Aylesbury, the paranoia and OCD issues. But after a few sessions we came to see a pattern throughout my life that started with the childminder's teenage son. I'd committed no violent acts before then; I had no anxiety before being half-strangled by him. Fear controlled my life and my mood from that day onwards. I went from a five-year-old victim to being beaten by racist bullies. I then grew tougher with my gang, but that same fear took over whenever I came across bullies or dangerous people, keeping me in a constant fight or flight mode. This came to ahead when I clashed with Wayne Lister, he was the real deal, a killer who could have killed me. I also had issues with self-identity due to being racially targeted as a child as well as from my mother's parenting. She kept me clean, fed me and we did family things together, but she was emotionally absent. She never said she loved me or hugged me. I grew to wander the streets, and by forming a gang it was like creating a replacement family, a band of brothers.

The more I delved into my past the more things made sense. That is what talking therapy does, it teaches you about your past and the reasons why things happened. After ten sessions I left it feeling better, boosted and positive. The improvements went on for a few years, but it stopped working. I still wasn't well, I had Daisy, but I still slept with a baseball bat close at hand. I was alert to everything around me. If I had a disagreement with someone over the slightest thing it would play on my mind. Or incidents from my past would replay over-and-over again. This is known as 'ruminating.' I could be getting on with the day but have these background thoughts which were usually around arguing with an old foe. It was mentally draining.

I went onto the internet and typed in my symptoms. It was the first time I'd come across complex post-traumatic stress disorder (CPTSD). I learned of treatment called eye-movement desensitisation and reprocessing (EMDR), about how it could help. I searched for a local therapist and arranged a consultation. We started from the beginning, and she noted the number of traumatic incidents in my past. She told me I was indeed suffering from CPTSD; that many incidents in my life may have caused it, mixed with not being protected as a child which left me lost. If you have zero protection and no safe place you are odds on to keep attracting traumatic events which then leads on to this condition. It had started at a young age and controlled my life. The therapist also believed that Wayne Lister staring in my eyes the way he did became a trigger for my uncontrollable violence afterwards. All of the fights I had when released from prison, the confrontations, it was because of those eyes. PTSD can be triggered by smells, noise and all sorts of other things.

I told her I'd done a lot of talking therapy and it was no longer helping. What I learned was that if you're suffering from PTSD your brain hasn't processed the memory of the trauma. That you are most probably so scared you freeze, and the memory gets stuck in a part of your brain called the amygdala, which causes the flashbacks as the memory plays over-and-over like a stuck record. Processed or long-term memories are stored in the hippocampus part of the brain.

So doing talking therapy may mean reliving a trauma many times over; but it doesn't really deal with the core problem. By doing eye-movements, which is what our eyes do when asleep, which creates dreams as we process information from the day, you can somehow process a traumatic memory, taking away the intense feeling of fear that is in your body, by moving it from the amygdala over into the hippocampus. This was to take away the feeling that was always in my chest, I could wake up in the middle of the night due to a trauma and have a feeling of the terror in it for days afterwards. No amount of talking therapy could take that away. EMDR gave me hope and I'll briefly explain the stages of this treatment.

*   *   *   *   *

Phase 1: History and treatment plan

My therapist looked deep into my early childhood and the rest of my life. She marked each trauma on a scale of one-to-ten, and we picked the ones that were higher up the scale to work on.

Phase 2: Preparation

She then taught me new ways to cope with the flashbacks and other psychological problems and the triggers I was experiencing. Somehow, to bring me back to reality and out of my hypervigilant state. Break the alertness and bring me back down to earth. Give my brain a rest from living in the past. This would be through mindfulness, involving meditation and deep breathing. I'd close my eyes and breath, release some of that tension in my chest. I then had to concentrate on what I felt protected by and that's when I burst out crying and sobbed like a little boy. It was horrible, I never felt protected by anyone or anything, ever! I still had that little boy deep within me, I was trying to heal him. I found it difficult, but I thought of a close friend who was big and strong mentally, who always had my back and I meditated on that as my protection.

I then had to meditate on wisdom, who gave me wisdom? Well, that was hard, because I didn't really look-up to many people for it but I managed to find something to meditate on. I then had to meditate on love, and that was easier. I thought of Daisy and my children which made me feel good. Then I'd finish off with a safe place, well I never felt safe so that was difficult, but I managed to find a photo of me on a beach where I looked happy, and I meditated on that. I'd repeat this process a few times for five minutes a day and it really did lower my stress levels.

Phase 3: Assessment

In the third phase of EMDR, my therapist identified my deepest memories that were to be targeted and all the associated problems like the physical sensations that were stimulated in my chest when I thought of the memory. The traumas that made me most uncomfortable we worked on with eye-movements.

Phases 4–7: Treatment

I was to do EMDR 2 which was a newer form of treatment for people experiencing CPTSD. It was more extreme. I stood in front of the therapist, took a deep breath and she would tell me to bring the memory up. Get a vision of it in my head, score the fear one-to-ten, which of course would be a ten. I wouldn't talk about it, the therapist didn't have to know the full details. For example, you could just say it was 'The man who attacked me.' I didn't have to give details of where, when or who that person was.

I'd tell her where the feeling of fear was in my body; then start the eye-movements. My therapist would put her finger in front of my face and move it left to right as I focused hard on the memory and the feeling in my body. Now with a normal person that has only ever experienced one trauma, they can process that horrific memory in a few sessions, bringing the stress level down. But for someone with CPTSD the traumas are so entwined and emotions all over the show, so a few sessions will not kick it.

Also, doing the basic looking left-to-right wasn't much use for me either, so my therapist moved her finger left-to-right, up-and-down and horizontally as I followed it with my eyes and focused on the memory and feeling. But it didn't stop there, as I was doing this, I held buzzers, one in each hand, that made a bleeping sound. I also did a V-step, I walked out to the right one step and back and then out to the left one step and back and then over to the right again repeating the process. This was scrambling my brain and the memory, but there was even more. While doing all of those movements I had to do times tables out loud, like the four times table backwards from 200, and I had to be able to do this and focus on everything. She said I was her only client who could do all of this together.

We stopped every few minutes and she would ask me to bring up the memory and give it a number from on-to-ten. Sometimes it was still ten and then we would repeat the process yet again. Eventually it would go down to seven or six. She would ask me where I had the feeling, or what shape it was in my chest. I'd sometimes say it was circle shaped and had got smaller. Or it had moved towards my neck. Instead of using the buzzers I'd then tap that area as I'd done in the other parts of the therapy. I'd find the feeling moved around and got smaller and smaller. Then it disappeared.

After a session I'd to do some form of exercise, so I'd go to the gym. With my brain scrambled it was horrible being in a packed place. My alertness was all over the place and I was drained. But then came the nightmares. As through EMDR you are processing the stuck trauma through the amygdala and into the hippocampus, your brain can take up to a week to process it and that doesn't stop at night. From 20 years of emotions linked with some traumas being processed in my brain I'd wake up in the middle of the night screaming in terror. 'Help, help' or 'Mum, Mum.' I was screaming out 'Mum' in my thirties. The dreams I had were disturbing, just imagine your worst experiences, thoughts, and feelings that you hid away all being mixed-up and blended together, only to find them start trying to come out in your dreams. They were dark and scary, but as time went on they became less so.

The sessions went on. I'd focus on being strangled by the childminder's son, or locked on the balcony and get the trauma down from a ten to a two or even one. Some memories just won't go down to one or zero. I'd try to go back to one, but it was scrambled. I couldn't see it or feel it. As I write this, I'm trying to find one in my chest but can't. So, it's gone into the hippocampus and is just like an ordinary or dull memory that doesn't mean anything. It doesn't cause me distress. But with a mountain of traumas there were and still are many to work on.

The memory of Wayne Lister was always going to a major one for me as it had caused me distress for over 15 years. I sometimes needed to remember how much the incident affected me. I'd go into the gym and pick up on a stare from someone, taking me back to the incident and I'd take the stare negatively. I'd be in fight mode and give off an aggressive vibe. But working on this memory, making it blur and bringing it right down, I no longer have a problem with people staring at me, I don't think I'm going to be attacked.

Recently I was on the tube and a man got on staring at me. Alarm bells rang as I picked-up on the bad vibes, he sat close to me and turned to me staring and staring. The old me would have got tense and looked back, but I didn't feel anything. I was aware of him and his bad vibes, but I took it like a normal person. Before, I'd have looked again-and-again until my hackles were up and if I was to say, 'You alright mate' that meant war. If his reply was, 'Yeah what, you alright' a confrontation could be on with a random stranger just like that. As if two aggressive dogs were sniffing each other in a park, any second it would go off. That was street life for you, but it happens in road rage too, if you're an angry or competitive driver you'll find someone just like you. I believe you attract what you think and what you are. But because of those EMDR sessions I saw the person staring at me as his problem not mine. I just looked straight on until he disappeared.

Phase 8: Evaluation

As we got deeper into the EMDR sessions something happened to the world. Oh yes, the bloody pandemic. This messed-up a lot of my recovery. We went from face-to-face sessions to online therapy which I hated. Instead of watching my therapist's fingers moving I had to place markers on the wall and look left to right at them. The thing is at my therapist's I felt safe. But in my own home it just wasn't the same. You are focusing on the darkest memories in your mind on your own, and then you are left alone. So, we did some sessions which were not as effective and though I hated them I carried on. Then my therapist caught Covid badly and my sessions stopped.

I haven't reached the end of Phase 8 and completed my EMDR. However, I am in a better place, I'm coping. I have a lot fewer flashbacks, and none of these are from the memories we worked on, only those that still need to be dealt with. But I can function more normally. I can go off to work, or out with my family and not feel as agitated, yet I'm far from cured. I doubt I'll ever be fully cured, I've just learnt to accept some of my issues. Others will always be a daily battle like my OCD, which got really out-of-hand in Aylesbury. That was because I'd lost control due to anxious and paranoid thoughts of Lister, so I was trying to take back a form of control in a strange way. The same as during my time as a gang leader experimenting with drugs, being around distressing situations, I was scared and losing control. I started believing seeing one magpie was bad luck, saluting it three times, or touching green for never seen, OCD in the making.

With Covid coming around and being told to wash our hands because of germs I took it to another level. I'd always have anti-bac with me ready to use after touching something I believed others had touched. Out shopping I'd pick up something from the back of the shelf, so I knew less people had touched it. If I touched a door handle, I'd think of that hand for an hour or two until I got to clean it and wash away potential germs or a person's energy. I realised that my OCD was getting extreme, so it is something I am still working on and with OCD it is best to face the rituals and horrible beliefs head on. For example, I don't wash my hands straightaway, live with the worry of someone's germs on them. I mean, I might be extremely uncomfortable, but I live with it. See that it isn't going to hurt me.

*   *   *   *   *

With this new attitude and less tension I believe I am more approachable, I notice more people talk to me when I'm out and about. I'm gentler so I attract more gentle things. But, of course, that wasn't always the case because being a young man with mental health issues can be extremely hard to just open-up about. To let your emotions show. I know too well that opening-up or showing kindness would have been seen as weakness when I was active on the streets.

I started with talking therapy and pushed that to my friends that were also going through trauma and some took it up. Now years down the line learning and doing EMDR I have pushed that to other friends who are now working on their traumas. Young men out there growing-up with mental health issues find it hard to talk about them, but if you keep them bottled-up it will usually end badly (I'd seen suicides many times in my late-teens and early-twenties, people close to me took their own lives, all young men). Some use drugs to cover over issues, others alcohol. I think reaching for help, standing-up to things and not being scared to do this can only be a good thing. With my reputation other men were shocked at how open I was; they felt they could relate to some of my mental issues no matter on what level.

Epilogue

I mentioned at the start of this book the sad loss of my close friend Joe Smith. There were others in my life who departed before their time, including my sister's boyfriend, Jay who became so desperate he took his own life. He'd been going through a rough time and suffered a breakdown. One night he checked into a hotel and hanged himself. It affected me quite badly. My old friend from Aylesbury, Fergus Tracy who I mentioned in *Chapter 3* went on to do the same in Belmarsh Prison, and a guy I knew around my manor, Scott, committed suicide in HMP High Down. I used to see him around the Sutton area, he had a street look about him and at first I'd stare him out. Then we got talking and became respectful. I saw through the street vibes and learned he was a good guy. Something else that affected me deeply was that a childhood friend and graffiti writer Jamaine (whose tag was 'Chez') also ended his own life.

Now what are these people? Statistics, memories. I often wonder if any of them sought help, whether it was talking or EMDR, and if they might be here today if they'd done so. I believe they would. The scariest thing about mental ill-health is if you don't know you have issues, or you hit a point like I did in Aylesbury when I was not in control of them.

I'm lucky to have made the long journey through different types of therapy and gained the knowledge of where my issues come from. EMDR has taken away threats from the world. I'm living proof of the benefits. I can see the light at the end of my own dark tunnel, and that's what I always tell others, to talk, open-up and face their fears. By doing this I gained a different sort of respect from people. Even rivals and enemies reached-out to me. I had one message from an old friend turned enemy who I'd hurt real bad in a fight, but he wrote the kindest of words telling me he wished me well and forgave me. Seeing this helped to change me as well.

Even though my daughter Gabriella's start wasn't the best I could give her she's turned into a gentle, loving girl. Things I couldn't do with her when she was young, I try to make sure I do with my younger daughter. Nowadays, when I take her, say, to a play centre, I'm the first dad going down the slide and so on. I think of how I couldn't do that with Gabriella and it upsets me. She's older now of course (and understands her dad has a past and had issues), clever and aware of everything around her, people's behaviour, their body language. She must have picked-up on that as a child from my more paranoid times, when I was on edge.

I no longer need to be a huge, fearsome figure like I did in my bodybuilding days, I feel healthier and more confident, being light and concentrating on cardio exercise which is brilliant for mental wellbeing. I've taught both my girls about positive thinking and self-belief. They signed-up with a modelling agency and have gone on to work with the biggest high street brands and top designers. They love it, having their hair done and (Covid permitting) getting to travel. Their money gets put aside for when they're older. Somehow, I produced two beautiful children and they don't have to go through the racial issues I did, first because the world has moved on slightly with races mixing more acceptably, but also because we finally traced our Sri Lankan roots and that began to heal this side of me in particular.

Remember back in *Chapter 6* when I met my Nathan and the Tamil boys in Aylesbury? As you know. I told Nathan I was Sinhalese. I didn't really have a clue what that meant or who I was. Probably the worst thing to say as Hindu Tamils were locked in a civil war with the mostly Buddhist Sinhalese. That war raged for nearly 30 years. It was even going on at the time when I met Nathan. What I didn't know was that I was from a Dutch Burgher family, from a small ethnic group in Sri Lanka, a mix of Dutch, Portuguese and British ex-pats. I hadn't a clue about my history, and I was beaten and called a 'Paki' during my childhood, taught to hate my race, when my family were not even what those bullies and racists perceived me to be. In fact, Dutch Burghers were quite high-class in Sri Lanka. My grandmother and her two sisters grew-up on their father's tea plantation in the capital, Colombo. Sri Lanka grows the best tea of course, even Twining's English Breakfast Tea is from there. My Nan and aunts attended private school, had English-sounding names, and even maids. It turns out they were Roman Catholics.

It was an emotional experience finding out about all this and more. My great grandmother was Ilene Cecilia Wallace and my great grandfather James

Edgar Woolfe, who owned a tea plantation. He'd sell his tea at the docks in Colombo way back in the mid-1800s, get talking to importers and buy jazz records from them. At home my Aunt Yolande would play the piano and sing along to them. Her surname was Bavan by marriage.

When Ceylon gained independence in 1948 it became known as Sri Lanka, and the language was changed to Sinhalese (also called Sinhala), leaving the Burghers in limbo. Many moved to England, Australia and Canada. Yolande Bavan sailed to Australia, aged 16, to be a pianist and two years later ended-up in England. I'd no idea but my relatives lived in St Johns Wood and other smart areas of London. Yolande attended jazz events, one day seeing Lambert Hendricks and Ross and getting to meet them, she knew every lyric of theirs off to a tee. When the group went back to America, Ross fell ill, and they needed a new female singer quickly. Their management suggested the exotic Sri Lankan girl they'd met in London.

Before she knew it Yolande was on a flight to New York and the group became Lambert, Hendricks and Bavan. She went on tour with many of the greats, like James Brown and she was friends with the legendary Louis Armstrong. She has wonderful photos of her and him. But her most notable friend was singer Billie Holiday. They became friends after Billie took my aunt under her wing due to her vulnerability in a foreign country. From what I know, Billie had a habit and didn't want Yolande to get involved in that side of the industry. Lambert, Hendricks and Bavan are nowadays in the Jazz Hall of Fame.

My Aunt Yolande is such a beautiful soul; we've been in contact for many years and meet up when she visits London. It was difficult for her to understand my behaviour or the places I'd been and seen. It affected her emotionally. My other aunt, Aunt Fleur is a beautiful soul too, so gentle and kind, a dietitian who owns her own clinic. She's also an author and lives a middle-class lifestyle in a house she built herself in leafy countryside. She adopted her two sons Tavi and Kirsten from orphanages in Thailand, and they have grown-up to be kind-hearted men. It says a lot when a woman does that, about how much love is in her heart.

Meeting Yolande and Fleur was a massive part of my healing process, I mean I used to cut my arms with razors out of the hate I had for myself but meeting them and learning about my family history taught me to love that side of myself. To be proud of my Asian roots, and it's even more exciting learning about them when it involves such a great story.

It took a long time to feel comfortable when people asked where I was from though. I'd spent so long on the wrong side of the tracks with little to be proud of other than my instinct for survival. Now, when I say I'm descended from 'Dutch Burghers' people perk up as they have often not heard of this before. Deep down I'll always be firstly British and a South Londoner though. It's where I grew-up and where my heart will always be. It's where my people, my community are, even though gentrification is in full swing and many older buildings are getting ripped down and nice apartments popping-up. The heart of London is still there, where cockneys, black people, white people, Asians and others now mix and flow together. I love that side of the city. That's where my own roots lie.

A few years back, I received a call to say my first book *The Lost Boyz* was going to be studied by students at Birmingham City University. I didn't really understand what this meant, but one of their academics who is now a regular TV presenter, criminologist Professor David Wilson, apparently saw something in my writing and thought his students could learn from it. The module was named 'On Crimes and Punishment: An Introduction to Criminological Theory.' I even became part of the question posed to students for their dissertation: 'Does Classicism or Positivism best explain why Justin Rollins committed crime?'

I was invited to visit the university as a guest speaker, not realising 500 undergraduates had been studying me. As I walked towards the lecture theatre, I noticed a queue of students waiting to enter. Shit, I was in panic mode, they were saying, 'Look there's Justin' and I didn't know where to turn. I went inside and stared up at the seemingly endless rows of seats as they filled with the first batch of 250 students. Professor Wilson said he couldn't believe the turnout, introduced me and we began.

At first, even though they had each read *The Lost Boyz*, I was nervous, but once I realised this was my life they were interested in, I thought 'Who better to talk about it than me?!' I relaxed and absolutely smashed it with my brutal honesty. I even made the room laugh. I felt like a musician must feel when they perform well on stage. Then there was a Q&A session when I told them to ask me anything at all, due to my belief in opening-up. The students warmed to this, it went down well, and afterwards I received a standing ovation, which I found overwhelming, hard to take. Before I knew it, they left and another 250 students piled in! They would all go on to write a long essay on my life. The whole thing went so well that another 500 studied my life the following year and in the years after that. I'd finally found my calling!

After that first lecture I sat in a pub with David Wilson and his colleagues and felt perfectly at ease talking and debating criminological theory with them. I'd always questioned my behaviour, and I had an understanding of the roads I'd taken. I analysed my street friends' behaviour, explained why people walked certain paths. I didn't want it to end, so I contacted other universities and went on to do talks across the UK. Now *The Lost Boyz* has become the core part of a module for students at Coventry University and recommended reading in other places of education. It has even been optioned for a movie and may yet reach the big screen. I've travelled the whole of Britain giving talks on criminology and youth offending. I'm sure I'll be taking *Mental Me* 'on tour' telling students about gangs, knife crime, childhood trauma, mental-illness and how I survived to be where I am today!

Reading over this book about the unstable young man I once was disturbs me greatly. What is written within these pages is extremely dark. I know *The Lost Boyz* was dark too, but I was just a boy in that book and, looking back, I'm rooting for that boy Justin to survive. But when I read this new book I really didn't like the character I saw. How can you warm to such a destructive soul, a disturbed thug? It's difficult reading about the tsunami of violence I dished out because today I'm completely anti-violence, the thought of street beef and fighting freaks me out. I don't want to see people hurt, I want to see them being happy.

One thing I also can't stand is how negative my frame of mind was and the warped mentality that made me think of myself as a victim. It's strange to read about that way of thinking. Yes, that's how I was, and maybe I was a victim at times but that doesn't excuse my actions, so I'm ashamed of that Justin Rollins. The scary thing is there are thousands of young men like that out there, unstable lost souls smashing their way through life.

You have to take responsibility for your actions to move forward. I have done some bad things in my life and do often wonder if my ongoing mental health issues are karma for my past actions. Nonetheless, you have to push forward somehow. The positive I can find from this writing is giving ordinary people who read my book a deep insight into that way of life. Above all, I hope it helps people that are going through difficulties mentally to go and seek help.

Index

Y
Yakuza *81*

Z
zombie *59*

Street Crhymes
Justin Rollins

Justin Rollins has a remarkable ability. His poems emerge not from agonising over a blank sheet of paper, but in full-flow and in their complete form. He deals with the everyday effects of disadvantage, the tensions of wealth and poverty, freedom and incarceration with glimpses of a sometimes dark past, motivational present and uncertain though optimistic future. What registers is Rollins' eye for detail, the telling remark, the eccentric, the absurd, clandestine places and parallel realities... The result is a raw journey captured in snapshots of street crimes, survival, pain and the author's travels on the London Underground.

'*Street Crhymes* reveals what goes on in the mind of a young offender, how they really feel and provides some real home truths about life behind bars'
David A Williams, Director of Youth Services, London Urban Arts Academy.

Paperback & Ebook | ISBN 978-1-904380-99-3 | 2013 | 168 pages

www.WatersidePress.co.uk

The Lost Boyz

A Dark Side of Graffiti

Justin Rollins

Foreword Noel 'Razor' Smith

A rare first-hand account of disaffected youth. Contains count-less lessons for young people who might be attracted to crime (and anyone involved with them socially or professionally).

'This is simply 100% raw talent being unleashed right from the start ...
This book is a must-read for the prison population, academics and politicians'
Inside Time

'An unforgettable story of a violent and disturbed young man, who, despite spiralling out of control, is anchored by his friendships and the power of his gang community.'
Social Work With Groups

Paperback & Ebook | ISBN 978-1-904380-67-2 | 2011 | 176 pages

www.WatersidePress.co.uk